On the Trail of the Poets of the Great War

ROBERT GRAVES &
SIEGFRIED SASSOON

On the Trail of the Poets of the Great War

ROBERT GRAVES & SIEGFRIED SASSOON

Helen McPhail
and
Philip Guest

Series editor
Nigel Cave

LEO COOPER

First published in 2001 by
LEO COOPER
an imprint of
Pen & Sword Books Limited
47 Church Street, Barnsley, South Yorkshire S70 2AS

ISBN 0 85052 838 0

A CIP catalogue record of this book is available
from the British Library

Printed by CPI UK

*For up-to-date information on other titles produced under the Leo Cooper imprint,
please telephone or write to:*

Pen & Sword Books Ltd, FREEPOST, 47 Church Street
Barnsley, South Yorkshire S70 2AS
Telephone 01226 734222

CONTENTS

INTRODUCTION BY SERIES EDITOR

Two figures have dominated the British literature of the Great War in the minds of the British public: Siegfried Sassoon and Robert Graves. Both of them were masters not only of prose but also of verse. Both were excellent self-publicists. Until the advent of television, their view of the war was the view that generations of school children were brought up with. Their 'memoirs' were the first two books that I read about the war, more years ago than I care to think about.

Extraordinarily enough, they were members of the same regiment – the Royal Welch Fusiliers. What is even more extraordinary is the other writers who also served with them at some stage or other in the same battalion of the regiment – Frank Richards, who wrote the great 'other rank' classic, *Old Soldiers Never Die* (though some have expressed the opinion that the book was in large measure ghosted by Graves) and Bernard Adams, who wrote that beautiful book, *Nothing of Importance*. It seems fairly certain that the writings of Sassoon and Graves inspired Captain J C Dunn to compile another Great War classic, *The War the Infantry Knew*, which is an account of the 2nd Battalion RWF, in which the two writers and Richards all served at some stage in the war. It was a reaction to the half truths and inaccuracies that were to be found in Sassoon's, and particularly Graves's, books.

Whatever the argument about the factual quality of the writings, these two authors produced deeply moving literary work about the Great War. No-one doubts the bravery and fighting record of both of them; and their writing reflects the reaction of men of their class and situation, though neither of them could be classed in any way as 'ordinary'. Helen McPhail and Philip Guest have produced a fascinating account of the military service of these men in the context of what may be seen today on the battlefields. When combined with visits to the deeply evocative cemeteries and the extant remnants of the battlefield, it provides another insight into two men who have been responsible for introducing the war to numerous readers and who have set the basis for many people's approach to that terrible conflict.

Nigel Cave
Derryswood
September 2001

INTRODUCTION

Both Robert Graves and Siegfried Sassoon presented the public with more than one version of their lives as officers in the First World War. Having written and published poetry during the war years, they both published prose accounts which began to appear ten years after the Armistice and which have remained in print ever since. Robert Graves's autobiography *Goodbye to All That* appeared in 1929 while Sassoon's thinly fictionalised autobiographical trilogy, *The Memoirs of George Sherston,* appeared as *Memoirs of a Fox-Hunting Man* (1928), *Memoirs of an Infantry Officer* (1930) and *Sherston's Progress* (1936).

From the 1940's Graves chose to suppress his war poems, which had to wait until after his death to be collected and published. By contrast, Sassoon continually revisited his wartime experiences and wrote a second trilogy, a straightforward autobiography which he called *Siegfried's Journey* and which was published in 1945 as *The Old Century, The Weald of Youth and Siegfried's Journey.* They met while serving together for a brief period in the same battalion of the Royal Welch Fusiliers, and their mutual delight at finding themselves in the company of a congenial fellow-writer in an alien and uncomfortable setting was the basis for a complex friendship in which each man both helped and hindered the other. Their similarities and differences continue to fascinate their readers, and both men have had a powerful influence on later attitudes to both the First World War itself and its literature. Although sickness and wounds took them out of the front line on several occasions, both had a long war service, shared many acquaintances and friends and, crucially, both were passionate about poetry.

If their two long lives were plotted on a single graph, the lines would come together in 1915 to be closely interwoven for three vital years with repeated encounters and very little divergence of attitude. Then, for a few years, the lines would veer away uncertainly from each other with occasional intersections, finally heading off in sharply different directions some ten years after the Armistice. Their post-war experiences, friendships and literary lives were so complex and wide-ranging that it is impossible to do them justice without plunging into a full biography. This guide, therefore, gives only the barest outline of the post-war years, together with a warm recommendation to read the work of these two remarkable and significant characters, and to pursue the fuller story of how their lives evolved.

Because of the way in which both Graves and Sassoon presented a subtle (and sometimes not so subtle) distortion of fact, character or interpretation, they have left a trail of misunderstanding which cannot always easily be disentangled. Even after reading Sassoon's diaries or the volumes of genuine autobiography, and the many accounts of Robert Graves's life, it is not always possible to disengage the reader's mind from what they chose to show us first of all - such is the vividness of their description, and the power of their poetry, that readers cannot help being drawn into the way they chose, or felt impelled, to present their individual pictures of life and death on the Western Front.

One of the factors that still brings the two men together in the public mind is the way in which they offered their lives to the outside world in the form of a fictionalised autobiography. Sassoon's 'Sherston' memoirs recount his childhood, young adulthood and war service in the form of a deceptively straightforward and highly sympathetic personal narrative, while Graves's *Goodbye to All That* is a brisk and highly entertaining account which describes the events of his life with more accuracy about his own personality than Sassoon in the form of Sherston - but which none the less distorts events and background in a way which earned him enduring distrust. In the case of both men, it is necessary to look carefully at the image of themselves that they chose to offer the world and then at the work of biographers and literary commentators before we can feel confident of achieving a true picture. Where Graves and Sassoon are concerned, a bibliography is a particularly important extension to the writers' own work (see page 187); and in both cases, this wider understanding gives added depth to their achievements. Their war experience was similar to that of many young men of their age and background, yet their writings and their highly personal and distinctive interpretations of the war have given us images of warfare that have outlived those of most of their contemporaries.

The poetry that Sassoon published during the war brought him great fame. Others had written verses imbued with despair but he was one of the first war poets to write with an incisive and satirical wit. For this reason he bewildered and indeed angered many of his readers, both military and civilian. Robert Graves's work as a war poet attracted much less interest. It was his *Goodbye to All That*, with its unforgettable picture of life in the trenches, that made him famous and which, like Sassoon's satirical verses, caused considerable offence. Their creations brought them fame and fortune, and it is probably fair to say that more people have become familiar with events in the First World War through the books of Graves and Sassoon than from almost any other source.

Helen McPhail, Philip Guest

ACKNOWLEDGEMENTS

Carcanet Press for permission to print extracts from *Goodbye to All That* (1929) and *Poems About War,* ed. William Graves, 1988.

Copyright of Siegfried Sassoon by kind permission of George Sassoon.

The Imperial War Museum for providing the group photograph at the 4th Army School at Flixécourt in which Siegfried Sassoon appears. Despite extensive efforts we have been unable to identify the copyright holder.

Hulton Getty for permission to reproduce the photograph of Siegfried Sassoon on p.13.

Dr Ian Kelsey Fry for permission to copy the photograph of his father Dr W. Kelsey Fry.

The Royal Welch Fusiliers Regimental Museum, Caernarfon for permission to use photographs of Colonels Stockwell and Garnett, and David E.Langley for providing the photographs and also for permission to use the photograph of the 3rd Battalion taken in 1915.

The Trustees of the Welch Regiment Museum of the Royal Regiment of Wales for permission to use the group photograph in which Lord Kensington appears.

The Syndics of Cambridge University Library for permission to use the photograph of David Thomas.

To Richard Perceval Graves for permission to reproduce the photographs of Robert Graves on pp 183 and 185 and an extract from *The Assault Heroic* and for biographical reference.

Messrs. Howard Minns and Albert Haworth for their help in locating Litherland Camp.

The Secretary of Formby Golf Club for permission to reproduce the photograph of the clubhouse.

Mr David Kelsall for permission to use the photograph of Lieutenant-Colonel Stanway.

Lieutenant-Colonel R.P. Pool for permission to use the photograph of 2nd Lt. V.F.Newton

Mr Keith Fuller of Sussex and Surrey Yeomanry Museum at Newhaven Fort for permission to use photographs of the Sussex Yeomanry in camp.

Mr C. Buckland of The London Stamp Exchange Ltd. for

permission to use photographs from their book *The Roll of Honour*.

Sefton Council for permission to reproduce the photograph of the Guard Mounting at Litherland Camp in World War 1.

Flintshire Record office of the Flintshire County Council for permission to reproduce the two photographs relating to Kinmel Park Camp

The Peninsular & Oriental Line Steam Navigation Company for permission to use the photographs of the SS *Malwa* and SS *Kashgar*.

Mr Robert Pike for permission to produce various battlefield and other photographs taken on behalf of the authors.

Mrs Jane Middlebrook for various information and permissions relating to her research concerning Siegfried Sassoon at Flixecourt Château.

The Trustees of the Estate of A.Guest for permission to use the photograph of the Lena Ashwell Concert Party 1918.

Lieutenant-Colonel (rtd.) R. J. M. Sinnett Royal Welch Fusiliers for various papers and information concerning the death in action of Lt. John B. Garnett and his Bren Gun Carrier crew at St. Floris in May 1940.

Mrs Margery Leeming for permission to photograph the Leave Pass signed by Robert Graves issued to her father during service with No. 16 O.C.B., Kinmel Park Camp.

Mr Richard Mellor, General Manager, African Trades of P & O Nedlloyd for permission to use his photograph of SS *Leasowe Castle* and for information on this vessel.

Charles and Lisbet Wheeler for the photograph of Weirleigh.

German PoWs bringing in wounded during the Battle of the Somme, 1916.

Chapter One

THE ROYAL WELCH FUSILIERS

The Royal Welch Fusiliers - the 23rd of Foot - and its numerous battalions have been part of the British Army's enduring traditions since the seventeenth century. Both Robert von Ranke Graves and Siegfried Loraine Sassoon in their various ways - sometimes controversial - contributed to this long and distinguished regimental history throughout their service during the Great War and afterwards.

Formed in 1688 (the regular British Army was established in 1661), the Royal Welch Fusiliers was promulgated as '23rd Regiment of Foot or Royal Welch Fusiliers'. Throughout the turbulent times of the 19th and 20th centuries the Royal Welch preserved its British Army seniority, somehow evading the upheavals of the years after the Second World War when regiments were disbanded or amalgamated despite bitter objection from the units involved. In the First World War, when the army included many young officers who were essentially 'civilians in uniform', their family and educational background encouraged this dedication to the well-established pattern of service and command.

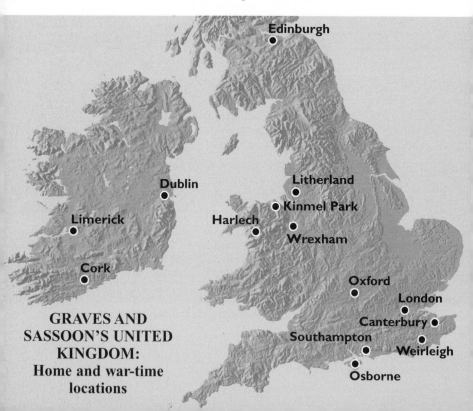

Edinburgh

Dublin

Litherland

Kinmel Park

Limerick

Harlech

Wrexham

Cork

Oxford

London

Canterbury

GRAVES AND SASSOON'S UNITED KINGDOM: Home and war-time locations

Southampton

Weirleigh

Osborne

The Regiment became a central part of the lives of both Graves and Sassoon, who fought with its 1st and 2nd (Regular) Battalions. In the spring of 1918 Sassoon also served with the 25th Battalion both in Palestine and France.

Robert Graves quickly fell under its spell as soon as he reached the Royal Welch's Regimental Depot shortly after arriving there in 1914 and Siegfried Sassoon was also conscious of the Regiment's sense of pride in its long and distinguished military past. This surfaced in later years when he objected to some of Graves's presentation, and encouraged him to contribute to Captain Dunn's unique record of the 2nd Battalion's service in the Great War.[1]

Siegfried Sassoon, photographed in 1915.

Robert Graves, a picture that he sent to his parents.

In accord with the times, there was also a certain degree of snobbishness in the battalion messes. This is visible in the case of two 23-year-old officers serving in the 2nd Battalion and both highly thought of as soldiers - Second Lieutenants Casson and Evans. Casson, educated at Winchester, fitted in well, while Evans was on attachment from the 7th (Merioneth and Montgomery) battalion and his background was apparently socially incompatible with the rest of the company mess. Such differences were ultimately pointless: on 26 September 1917 both men were killed in action near Black Watch Corner in the Ypres Salient. Even in December 1916, after the Somme battles in which so many of the 'amateurs' had given their lives, there was agitation in the Regiment over a proposal to admit men who had enlisted for 'the duration' to membership of the Regimental Comrades Association. The two regular battalions were adamantly opposed to the suggestion.

As the war progressed, both Sassoon and Graves had reservations over the way it was

[1] *The War the Infantry Knew* – see bibliography, p.187

managed, and expressed unflattering opinions of their superiors, until regimental pride and its sense of family eventually won them over. One consequence was that during the Second World War Robert's son David followed in his father's footsteps: he too was commissioned in the Royal Welch, only to be lost in 1943, fighting bravely with its 1st Battalion in Burma. By an odd coincidence, the date of his death, 18 March, was the same as the date of death of David Thomas (after who he was named) in 1916. The entry against his name in the Rangoon Memorial Register is `Son of Captain Robert Graves formerly of The Royal Welch Fusiliers......'

A VERY LITERARY REGIMENT

The First World War has left us many famous literary names representing many famous regiments and battalions, but it seems unlikely that any could claim a greater number of poets and writers than the Royal Welch Fusiliers. Like Graves and Sassoon, Bernard Adams, the author of *Nothing of Importance,* served with the Regiment's 1st Battalion on the Western Front until he was mortally wounded in February 1917. David Jones, poet and painter, who in 1937 wrote the remarkable prose-poem *In Parenthesis*, had considerable service with the Royal Welch's 15th Battalion (London Welch) and took part in the terrible fighting in Mametz Wood in July 1916 (where he was wounded), the aftermath of which involved both Graves and Sassoon. (Sassoon and David Jones met and talked at length at a literary society dinner in 1964, but although Sassoon considered *In Parenthesis* an important account of the Great War, he thought Jones himself to be `ultra sensitive'. Presumably the writing styles of the two men were too dissimilar for Sassoon to appreciate more than the descriptive elements of Jones's long narrative). The writer and later broadcaster, Captain Llewellyn Wyn Griffith, author of *Up to Mametz,* was originally with the London Welch. He later served as a Staff Officer during the fighting in Mametz Wood, where his brother Private Watcyn Griffith was killed in action.

The time-serving soldier and reservist, Private Frank Richards, DCM, MM, served with the 2nd Battalion and in 1933 wrote the much-acclaimed *Old Soldiers Never Die*. A different type of record of service in the RWF, which has been studied with care and enthusiasm over the years since its publication in 1938, is J. C. Dunn's *The War the Infantry Knew*, a compilation, with editorial comment, of extracts from some of these books together with other accounts of the Regiment's war.

In August 1914 the regiments of the British Expeditionary Force went to France, a small but magnificent and highly trained body of men that included the 1st and 2nd Battalions of the 23rd of Foot. The battle experiences of these two battalions in the early days of the war and their consequences had a great bearing on the subsequent welcoming atmosphere when Graves and Sassoon joined them. Fate initially dealt with these two battalions very differently and the memory of their war service with the Regiment with its humour and its pain was to be with Graves and Sassoon throughout their lives.

With the need to provide garrisons at many places overseas, each regiment maintained a minimum of two regular battalions, one of which was stationed at home in the United Kingdom whilst the other carried out its duties in various countries in what was then known as the British Empire. It so happened that at the outbreak of war on 4th August 1914 the 2nd Battalion Royal Welch Fusiliers had recently returned from abroad and was in training at Bovington Camp, near Wool in Dorset. It was therefore quickly available for service overseas. The 1st Battalion, however, formed part of the Malta garrison and, although it was immediately ordered back to England, it was almost a month before the troops could embark on a Cunard liner taken up by the War Office to carry them to Southampton, where they arrived on 16th September.

There were other arrangements to be made concerning the Royal Welch. The 3rd (Reserve) Battalion had been in south west Wales operating away from the Regimental Depot and Headquarters at Wrexham, but four days after the Declaration of War the Battalion was back at its Headquarters receiving the large number of reservists recalled to the colours. So great were the numbers that the barracks

The British Army arrives in France. Men of the first contingent to reach France on 7 August 1914.

there proved inadequate and tents had to be erected on the football field at the rear of the barrack blocks. Even so Frank Richards and some of his friends in the Reserve had to sleep on the barrack square.

On 10 August 1914 the 2nd Royal Welch, now up to a strength of 29 officers and over a thousand men, set off for France. The Regimental Goat traditionally borne on the Battalion's roster was not with them, having died just before the declaration of war; one of the Company Sergeant Majors later suggested that 'it must have known something'.

As generally anticipated, the port of departure was Southampton, but despite their presumptions that the Channel crossing would be made in the luxury of a Cunard liner, the War Office had laid on a former Irish cargo ship whose normal route was the transport of pigs between Ireland and Holyhead. On reaching Rouen during the evening of the next day the battalion was told that they were to be Lines of Communication troops and eventually to be part of 19th Brigade, an independent formation to be called into action only when necessary. With hindsight this was to be a lucky appointment, for as the war progressed the 2nd Royal Welch were seldom called upon for major actions prior to the Somme battles, with the result that casualties tended to be light. (Indeed, whilst carrying out an inspection in March 1916, Lieutenant-General Sir Richard Haking, commanding the Corps, remarked on the pleasure it gave him to review a battalion with such a high proportion of regular soldiers in its ranks).

On 12 August 1914 parties from the battalion took post in Amiens, which had been designated as a British Advanced Base. The

British troop transports on their way to Rouen. The 2nd Royal Welch disembarked at Rouen on 10 August 1914.

Commander of the British Expeditionary Force, Sir John French, set up his Headquarters here, in the Hotel du Rhin not far from the railway station and for whom they were expected to mount a guard. (Sassoon later became a frequent visitor to this hotel and others in the town.) On their arrival in Amiens the 2nd Royal Welch were immediately allocated a Corporal in the French Army whose duty it was to act as battalion interpreter; they were impressed to find that he was a French duke.

The following day a formation of Royal Flying Corps aircraft left England for Amiens. When resuming the journey three days later, an aircraft of No. 3 Squadron unfortunately stalled on take-off and crashed to the ground, killing Second Lieutenant E.W.C.Perry and Air Mechanic 2nd Class H.E.Parfitt who was with him. A military funeral took place at St. Acheul French National Cemetery in Amiens, with the Prefect of the French Department, the Mayor and a battalion of a French Territorial regiment taking part. The 2nd Royal Welch supplied a firing party at the burial service. Second Lieutenant Perry was the first British officer to be killed on active service in France during the Great War.

The Commander-in-Chief, Sir John French, arrived at Boulogne, France, 14 August, 1914.

The 2nd Royal Welch's detachment, now grown in size to almost half the Battalion, was also responsible for meeting the trains that passed through Amiens on their way to the front and for supplying the hungry troops with food and water. On 17 August a Guard of Honour

Amiens, the Hotel du Rhin today. A popular lunch-time venue for officers of the 2nd RWF in the Great War, it was also remembered as the Headquarters of Sir John French, Commander in Chief BEF, in August 1914. The battalion was detailed to furnish a guard at the hotel while he was in residence.

The graves of 2nd Lieutenant Perry and Air Mechanic 2nd Class Parfitt, Royal Flying Corps, who were killed when their aircraft crashed on 16 August 1914, lie in the shade of the tree in the centre. Troops of the 2nd RWF assisted at the interment. The graves beyond the tree commemorate some of the hundreds of French soldiers who died in the fighting around Amiens and those of some Belgian soldiers are visible to the left.

supplied by the 2nd Royal Welch met an incoming train to remove the body of the Commander of II Corps, Lieutenant-General Sir James Grierson, who had died suddenly during the journey.

Lieutenant-General Sir James Moncrieff Grierson died 17th August 1914.

Grierson's death had considerable repercussions, for he was immediately replaced by Sir Horace Smith-Dorrien – not the first choice of Sir John French, the Expeditionary Force's commander. There was, moreover, a clash of personalities between Sir Horace and his superior. Despite French's apparent initial approval for Smith-Dorrien's handling of the battle at Le Cateau on 26 August during the retreat from Mons, the relationship did not improve and Smith-Dorrien eventually resigned his command in May 1915.

Part of the uniform worn by a Royal Welch Fusilier is 'the Flash', a five-tailed flash of black silk ribbon attached to the tunic collar, a relic of the days when wigs were abolished and a fashion then developed of tying the hair up in a queue. The privilege of wearing the Flash is jealously guarded by the Regiment, although in 1907 Sir John French instructed that it should be removed from the uniforms of the 1st Battalion when they were serving under him at Aldershot. The 2nd Battalion disregarded the command, persuading themselves it did not apply to them as they were on active service in India at the time Sir John French gave the order. There was some concern now that Sir John, using the Hotel du Rhin in Amiens as his headquarters, might notice that the Flash was still being worn at the guard mounting outside his hotel. In the event, Sir John had more important things to concern him and as he strode by treated the guard commander to just a gracious smile.

The detachment's stay in Amiens was soon curtailed. Forming up in the forecourt of the railway station on 22 August, they boarded a long troop train to join the rest of the 2nd Royal Welch who had come from Rouen, the whole Battalion eventually arriving in a position a few miles south of Mons.

By now the pressure on the Allied armies on all fronts was increasing and soon afterwards, on 31 August, Amiens was captured by the Germans. This was a great military success for the German army, for the town lay at the junction of several vital roads and railway lines, but fortunately it was recaptured by the French on 13 September.

After taking part in the retreat from Mons to the Marne and the subsequent advance to the Aisne, the 2nd Royal Welch was redirected to the Ypres salient and reached Vlamertinghe by 16 October 1914. The 2nd Royal Welch's second in command, Lieutenant-Colonel O. de L. Williams, who took over from Lieutenant-Colonel Delmé-Radcliffe, the pre-war Commanding Officer who left for home after suffering a nervous breakdown, was to command the battalion until May 1916, when he was promoted to the rank of Brigadier-General. On reporting to the battalion in the summer of 1915 Graves took a dislike to Colonel Williams (entirely unjustisfied, according to others). Never the less, when looking back upon their service with each of the two regular battalions, both Sassoon and Graves preferred the time that they spent with the 1st Battalion.

Casualties in the fighting around Ypres between 19 October and 22 November - known as 'First Ypres' - totalled some 58,000: the B.E.F which had set out so bravely in August 1914 was now a shadow of its former strength. It is estimated that by the end of November of that year, in each battalion that had been involved in the fighting,

The Prime Minister in France, Herbert Asquith (with Sir John French on his right) receiving high-ranking Allied Staff Officers. Note the smart turn-out of the sentry on duty, who is extending military courtesies to the visiting officers by 'presenting arms'.

19

Occupied Amiens, 1914: German infantry marching through Amiens on 31 August. One soldier has apparently fallen out of column, and two women bend over him.

perhaps only one or two officers and just over a score of Other Ranks remained of those regulars and reservists who had landed in France so cheerfully in the summer. The 1st Royal Welch were no exception, and indeed both battalions needed reinforcements. (A similar fate befell the 1st Royal Welch in the fighting of May/June 1940, when only a small number of men managed to reach Dunkirk for evacuation and return to England.)

The view from beside the railway station, showing a battery of German artillery evacuating the city at the end of their army's ten-day occupation. The prominent building on the left is the Hotel Belfort, Sassoon stayed here on 30 March 1917, occupying a room with a balcony from which he could see the station. His diary records a notable dinner with fellow-officers in the city.

Chapter Two

TWO NEW OFFICERS

Very strong feelings about the war had prompted both Sassoon and Graves to join the army, and in just over a week from the declaration of war on 4 August 1914 both men were with their chosen units in training. The following year would see both of them embark on active service with the Royal Welch. Although there were similarities in the backgrounds of these two subalterns who joined the Royal Welch Fusiliers in the autumn of 1915, since both were born into educated and cultured families which took intellectual interests and artistic creativity as a normal feature of life, considerable differences in age and family style divided them.

Siegfried Loraine Sassoon was the elder of the two, born on 8 September 1886 into a household which combined traditional English country life with a successful Jewish merchant family. After his parents' separation when he was very small, he and his two brothers Hamo and Michael lived with his mother in the beautiful landscape of rural Kent. Mrs Sassoon, born Theresa Thornycroft (depicted as 'Aunt Evelyn' in her son's fictionalised memoirs), was cultured and loving - and also artistic, using a large studio in the garden for her painting; her brother Hamo Thornycroft was a well-known sculptor. Young Siegfried grew up with poetry and art as part of his daily life throughout a sheltered childhood, blending with his twin passions for riding and cricket. Formal education appears to have been conventional, but

Weirleigh, a modern view. The wing to the left, which overlooks the steep approach road, originally had a tall turret that further asserted the house's dominating position.

although he saw himself as a poet (and published slim volumes of verse at his own expense), profound intellectual application was not a natural element of his character.

It is part of the problem of disentangling fact from fiction that through the vision of late Victorian and Edwardian England, so beguilingly and nostalgically described in *Memoirs of a Fox-Hunting Man* with its persuasive images of childhood and adolescence, Sassoon manages to conceal his true self behind the appearance of straightforward memory. This backward view is so heartfelt, bathed in the afterglow of a romanticised golden age, that from the age of 40 when he wrote it he easily draws the reader into these idyllic surroundings seen from the far side of his adult experience and the First World War.

Robert von Ranke Graves, born on 24 July 1895, was to give a much harsher view of his own upbringing as part of a large family in Wimbledon, with a total of ten children from two marriages. His father, Alfred Perceval Graves, was both a poet and a member of the national school inspectorate whose first wife died in 1886, leaving him with five children. His second wife was a German connection by marriage, Amalie von Ranke, with whom he had five more children, Robert being the third. Both the English and the German sides of his family represented intellectual interests and the liberal professions, with lawyers, writers, doctors, the Church, the navy and the army all represented. In *Goodbye to All That* Robert gives a somewhat unfair image of his parents, who were endlessly helpful and concerned - reasonably so, in view of the events, personalities and attitudes involved - but sometimes exhausting when Robert was struggling to find both his emotional equilibrium and his voice as a poet. His mother, to whom Robert remained devoted and who made high demands on her family in terms of morality and thought, was endlessly available to support her difficult warrior-writer son. She and Alfred were always ready to visit, support, take an interest, advise. It is possible that Robert Graves's need for a female focus for his devotion, throughout his post-war life, was a consequence of the relationship with his mother. Calls on his parents' financial support were many when Robert was making his way as a poet and thinker, although he was clearly unhappy at being dependent on his father's financial generosity in the 1920s.

Throughout his life Robert seems to have been inclined to behave rather like a disaffected adolescent, and the tone of *Goodbye to all That*

- describing a period when he was not long past his school-days - often reflects this style of approach. Both parents were in their forties when Robert was born, and he writes of finding it easier to get on with them on account of this considerable age-gap than if they had been younger. His father was extremely heavily occupied in school term-times, as an inspector of schools in Southwark, and his mother had many domestic and social obligations - but both were very attentive to their children's upbringing and their moral and intellectual education. According to one biographer, writing just before Graves's death:

> *From the Graves side of his family, Robert has inherited charm, warmth, good-humour, a bad business sense, a great love of words, a seemingly endless capacity for hard work, enormous pride, great sensitivity, an occasional cool arrogance, and a brain so quick and changeable that half-finished sentences are left abandoned and forgotten in mid-air.*[2]

The somewhat puritanical idealism that he inherited from his mother was combined with the inheritance, from one or other parent and from an early age, of a deep passion for the use, interpretation and flavours of language.

Even more fully than Sassoon's evocation of his hesitant and instinctively nostalgic approach to life, Graves reveals a combative and thin-skinned boy, intelligent, passionate in his likes and dislikes, intolerant and ambitious. While Sassoon spent his time doing his best to get on with others, hero-worshipping a thoughtful groom or a talented village cricketer, Graves was more inclined to distrust authority and consider himself at least as good as anyone else.

Both boys were sent as a matter of course to well-known public schools - Sassoon to Marlborough College, where he failed to shine, and Graves to Charterhouse, where he struggled to conform but was difficult and unhappy. The differences between their accounts of adolescence are revealing: Sassoon, in both the 'Sherston' books and in his genuine autobiography, shows himself as confused and unsuccessful in academic terms, unconcerned about scholastic achievement, and notably unable to apply his mind consistently: throughout his life he seems to have been driven more by instinct than by rationality. After leaving school in 1904 he needed extra tuition to gain entrance to Cambridge University then, having won a place, failed to stay the course and finish his degree. He seems to have been torn between two instincts - to become a poet and enter London society with its many opportunities of social and cultural life or to be a regular

[2] *The Assault Heroic, 1895-1926*, Richard Perceval Graves

golfing, hunting and cricketing country gentleman. Friends in both worlds provided hospitality and friendship, social and cultural life, invitations or horses: but he was lonely - in London he was not wealthy, bold or talented enough to make his way as a poet or 'man about town' and in the country he realised that, despite successes on the hunting-field and in amateur racing, and his deep delight in landscape and nature, there was more to life than immersion in rural life. Another great enthusiasm was anything to do with cricket: it was a life-long passion which brought him some outstanding and enduring friendships. This understanding of rural life is visible throughout his prose writing and underlies many poems about the settings that became familiar along the Western Front.

In the summer of 1914 the 27-year-old Sassoon still felt uncertain about his future. The outbreak of war seemed a solution to the age-old problem - what to do with his life. He was living beyond his means, doubtful of his abilities as a poet, at a time when the news and talk in late July were all about the threat of war: volunteers would be required. He responded to the call, satisfying his country's need and his own at the same time. The First World War changed everyone's life, and Sassoon's was no exception. In his case, it brought him to a late maturity, a break from emotional dependence on his mother, contact with an influential group of figures on the national scene - and gave him his true voice as a poet.

Robert Graves, meanwhile, came to the war in different style, as a much younger man - but for him too, the war presented itself as the solution to a moment of indecision and unease. He had responded to his parents' urgings towards academic excellence, gaining a very sound classical education as well as sporting prowess. (Outside school, he was an excellent skiier and rock-climber.) In *Goodbye to All That*, Graves writes with considerable bitterness about his life at Charterhouse; although he made satisfactory reasonable academic and sporting progress, he ran into deep personal problems with religious doubts (his Christian faith wavered, although spiritual belief was always important) and also over his intense friendship with a younger boy.

In contrast to Sassoon's emotional ties with home, Graves resented the continuing lack of freedom of thought that was imposed on him. Poetry was a welcome distraction and he wrote steadily: in his final year the extra time gained by permission to abstain from military drill - ostensibly in order to spend more time on working for his university scholarship examination - was often used for writing poetry or attempts at journalism. More public efforts at writing and studying poetry came to grief when the school magazine, *The Carthusian*, published some apparently innocent unsigned poems that were shown to conceal references of spiteful personal innuendo; members of the Poetry Society were involved, Robert Graves incautiously revealed names and the Society - which had been a source of solace to him in wretched moments - was dissolved.

One of the best aspects of school life was his friendship with George Mallory, a young teacher who took an interest in this awkward but interesting pupil and introduced him to modern authors of the day - Shaw, Rupert Brooke, H.G. Wells, John Masefield and others. Mallory, a keen climber who was later lost on Everest, thus contributed to his true literary education and encouraged the youth in a sense of his own worth as a writer. Poems that have survived from this period show a growing interest in magic or myth - the area in which he made a distinguished name in later years with his work on the White Goddess.

Robert Graves's happiest moments were spent on holiday with relatives in north Germany and near Harlech, in North Wales, in the family holiday house 'Erinfa'. The area became a haven of escape from the rigidities of home and school (and, later, from adult worries) where the Graves children were free to roam widely and explore the magnificent mountain scenery. Although he fulfilled his parents' hopes and expectations by winning a place at St. John's College, Oxford, he could not feel fully committed to the prospect. The intensive atmosphere of a classically-based education in the Edwardian traditions of an old-fashioned English public school had left him highly trained in the ancient classics, an accomplished versifier - and clumsy, brash, unpopular, and unprepared for adult life.

Kitchener's famous recruiting Call to Arms, 'Your King & Country Need You', was in all British newspapers on the morning of 7 August 1914, but Sassoon had anticipated the call. Rapidly passed medically fit for service, by 3 August he had been embodied in the British Army and was wearing the uniform of a trooper in the Sussex Yeomanry, a Territorial Force cavalry unit.[3] His favourite horse, Cockbird, was with him.

To an accomplished horsemen who wanted to serve in the army, a Yeomanry regiment would appear to be an ideal choice for Sassoon. However, although many of the regiment came from a social class with which Sassoon could readily identify, he chose to enlist in the ranks rather than seeking a commission; he seems to have deliberately avoided the responsibility of officer status without realising that this

[3] The rank of Trooper was not used by the Sussex Yeomanry during the Great War, the title for such a man at that time being Private soldier. It has been convenient, however, to use the post-war description Trooper for a cavalryman. Similarly, the title Private soldier has been used in the text whenever reference is made to a soldier of that rank in the Royal Welch Fusiliers although in later years he would have been referred to as Fusilier.

A group of Non-Commissioned Officers of the Sussex Yeomanry in camp 1914.

would cut him off from companionship in a period when social barriers were very strong. In addition, it is surprising that a man of Kent, so devoted to his own county, was attracted to neither the Royal East Kent Yeomanry nor the West Kent Yeomanry (Queen's Own).

In the event Sassoon was soon back in Kent, for although he was initially garrisoned at Lewes with his squadron, the whole regiment was quickly moved to Canterbury where it spent the next twelve months. (Like the Sussex Yeomanry, both regiments eventually formed part of the South Eastern Mounted Brigade landing at Helles, Gallipoli in October 1915 to take part in that terrible campaign - but fate took Sassoon in a different direction and by that time he was already safely in England serving as a Second Lieutenant with the Royal Welch Fusiliers.)

Officially speaking, Sassoon's unit was the 1/1st Sussex Yeomanry, designated to fight as cavalry and trained entirely with that aim in mind. Ironically, however, these squadrons of skilled horsemen of all

The Sussex Yeomanry in camp, 1914, at Lewes. Siegfried Sassoon joined the regiment here in 1914.

ranks, many of them, like Sassoon, with their own horses brought into the regiment, were destined never to fight in a mounted role. (With the rapid war-time expansion of the army, the regiment formed two additional units, the 2/1st and 3/1st Sussex Yeomanry.)

THE LAST CAVALRY CHARGE

In 1941 the Sussex Yeomanry were still acting as dismounted troops and were in action as gunners taking part in the campaign in Eritrea against Italian forces. On one occasion they were astonished to see a troop of about 60 horses being ridden at full gallop towards them. The Italian cavalrymen were no match for the battery of 25 pounder guns of the Sussex Yeomanry brought to bear at point blank range upon the riders and horses charging at them. Many were killed. The incident is now recorded as the last time that the British Army was on the receiving end of an enemy cavalry attack.

For all arms - infantry, cavalry etc - farms were recognised as suitable places in which to lodge formations of troops, with grazing for the horses, perhaps some stabling, and ample, although possibly uncomfortable, accommodation in the barns and outbuildings for the men. Arriving in Canterbury, Sassoon's squadron was established at Hoath Farm where troop, squadron, regimental and brigade training began. Horses were in short supply, although many in the regiment had brought suitable horses from their own stables, just as Sassoon had brought his favourite horse Cockbird (on which he had won a point-to-point, an event described memorably in *Memoirs of a Fox-Hunting Man*). This arrangement was by no means unusual. Edward Horner, brother-in-law of Raymond Asquith - one of the sons of Herbert Asquith, the Prime Minister - was most anxious to enlist and when on the outbreak of war he set off to join the North Somerset Yeomanry, his local Territorial Force regiment, he took his sister's two best horses with him. He was also accompanied by his valet and a cook. Whether

Hoath Farm, Canterbury, 1914. Men of the Sussex Yeomanry were taken off normal duties to make camp roads.

Hoath Farm - the stables of No. 4 Troop, AB Squadron, Sussex Yeomanry, taken in 1915.

or not these two servants genuinely wished to join the army is not clear!

'Horse-collecting parties' were sent out to scour the countryside, in competition with other similar groups urgently seeking horses to commandeer for the British Expeditionary Force abroad. On several occasions men of the regiment departed to collect suitable mounts only to discover that they had already been marked down for other units, forcing them to return with the halters but no horses. The Field Artillery was always a strong competitor. Throughout the war artillery regiments were permanently short of horses, for of necessity these hard-worked animals, sometimes poorly fed and usually in open horse lines, had to work under fire and often became casualties. The wastage was high.

Nor was the life of a cavalry trooper's horse an easy one, a fact that Sassoon soon recognised: his much-loved Cockbird, a fine hunter, was

British Army horses - a squadron of lancers on the move in France, in 1914, illustrating the amount of equipment carried by cavalry horses. Late in the war, the issue of gas masks and steel helmets to cavalrymen added to the burden.

unsuited to carry the weight of a trooper's equipment and had to be sold to his squadron for an officer's use.

CAVALRY KIT

The cavalry horse was required to carry his rider in full uniform with his lance or sword, rifle and rifle bucket and/or revolver and holster, webbing equipment to which was attached his 'small pack' containing shaving gear etc, mess tins and personal gear, water bottle, bayonet frog and bayonet. The cavalryman also wore extra bandoliers containing a total of 140 rounds of ammunition and, as squadrons were not provided with Field Kitchens, he was also supplied with a sandbag full of rations. Where it was likely that the troop would be operating on a dismounted duty, a pick and/or shovel was also provided.

The horse was also expected to carry another bandolier, (its pockets containing around 90 rounds of rifle ammunition), usually slung across its neck, a canvas water bucket, a saddle blanket and one for the cavalryman. Two leather wallets were slung over the saddle to carry the trooper's spare pair of boots, emergency rations and a number of hand grenades. The sword case also held extra horseshoes, measured to fit, together with shoe nails, girth band and picketing peg. Feed for the horse - a bag of oats and a net containing hay - was also carried. The weight represented by this list gives an indication of why Sassoon was concerned for his hunter's well-being.

Sassoon was not a natural private soldier: although a skilled sportsman he was not physically practical, nor was he accustomed to the timetable and routines of the soldier's life. He was chafing at the conditions when circumstances early in his regimental training brought relief, in the form of a heavy fall while schooling one of the squadron's chargers - a severely fractured right arm kept him away from full regimental duties for some three months. It also spared him from external work for, as with many units, men of the Sussex Yeomanry were liable to be taken off training to serve as working parties, helping the War Office contractors to build huts and stabling. (The Regimental History reports that some of these 'were probably the first and possibly the worst huts erected in England for the accommodation of troops.')

Territorial Forces could not be required to serve abroad without their consent but, with the War Office in need of men to send overseas, Commanding Officers were instructed to call for volunteers. If 80 per cent or more came forward, the unit could be trained swiftly and sent abroad. This was recognised as unfair to men who had signed up as territorials but who had heavy civilian commitments at home and the Sussex Yeomanry did not meet the requisite quota, although Sassoon, with no serious domestic commitments, was ready and anxious to serve overseas. Later the quota was reduced by a further 20 per cent, and with the Sussex Yeomanry easily meeting this threshold they departed overseas in 1915 for service in Gallipoli. (Ironically, in 1914 the Remount Service, a 'safe' posting where his knowledge of horses would have been invaluable, had offered him immediate promotion to the full rank of captain, a rank he did not achieve until the end of his war service and subsequent demobilisation.) The educational calibre of Other Ranks in the Sussex Yeomanry, together with their pre-war and current military training, made them highly suitable for the increasing number of officers required for Kitchener's New Army, but Sassoon had already decided to leave the Yeomanry in order to seek overseas action.

During his period of convalescence, happily at home in Weirleigh, he was able to write poetry once more. The experience of life in the army had evidently helped his ideas and attitudes to develop, as he was able to distance himself in a more adult way from his mother; and even while his work from this period reflects his straightforward delight in the fine early spring weather, it also shows greater maturity. He had also benefited from literary advice, specifically from Edward Marsh.

EDWARD MARSH

Edward Marsh (1872-1953), a leading member of the contemporary London world, appealed naturally to Sassoon's juvenile style and at this stage was highly constructive in encouraging him to focus his thinking more clearly and write in a more restrained manner. Well connected socially and politically, Marsh was the editor of the Georgian Poetry collections of pre-1914 modern poetry; the work that he published began by being innovative but finally reflected Marsh's own conservative instincts too closely to keep up with post-war literary developments. Suspicious of advanced experiment in writing, he none the less encouraged the Georgian poets in their search for natural tone and style, and simple language in contrast to high Victorian style and heavily classical reference, and was a friend of Rupert Brooke, among others. In another direction, he was Private Secretary to Winston Churchill. When Sassoon was uncertain about the direction of his life, it was Marsh who encouraged him to move to London, although the experiment proved too costly for Sassoon's carefully managed allowance.

It seems that Sassoon consulted a local family friend in Kent about his next step and, with a suitable written recommendation to support his application, he was granted a commission as a Special Reserve officer in the Royal Welch Fusiliers with seniority from 28 May 1915. In a period of strict social barriers, an officer in the Special Reserve was considered superior to his equivalent in Kitchener's Army. Part of the wide-reaching restructuring carried out by Richard Haldane, Secretary of State for War between 1906 and 1912, had been the reorganisation and renaming of the Militia whose history can be traced back to 1685 and the Monmouth Rebellion. This ancient lineage carried a certain social cachet and, together with the pedigree of the Royal Welch - 23rd Foot - Sassoon must have felt pleased with the success of his application. Despite his limited funds, he immediately went straight to the best military tailors he could find, to order his officer's uniform - very like kitting himself out with hunting clothes.

He left for France on 17 November 1915.

In July 1913, Robert Graves attended his school Corps camp on Salisbury Plain, and was surprised at the display of fortifications and weaponry. In a school debate, most of his school-fellows were fully convinced of the national need to defend their country, but Graves spoke out against the waste of educated men being engaged in war. During this school year he won an Exhibition (a minor award) to Oxford but in the following term he was forced to resign from editorship of *The Carthusian* after publishing some highly critical remarks about the school in the guise of a parody letter. According to later report, Graves declared at this stage in his life that only poetry and 'Peter' Johnstone, the object of his affections, really mattered. However, over the Easter holidays in 1914 he won plaudits and enthusiasm for his prowess at boxing, and spent ten days climbing in Snowdonia with George Mallory. His final term at Charterhouse ended, perhaps characteristically, in a flurry of fighting (literally and metaphorically), a near-scandal, and continuing discord.

Graves was a few days past his nineteenth birthday when he left school, uneasy at the prospect of three years at Oxford, and dreaming of life as a writer. As a biographer has noted, he was;

> *a good friend, a fierce enemy, always prepared to modify his views when he heard a better argument than his own, but steadfast in his opinions when he did not; easy to please but quick to take offence; usually ready with a smile and a warm handshake, but occasionally just as ready with his clenched fists ...*[4]

Robert's German-born mother was deeply distressed by the outbreak of war, and Robert, bitterly opposed to war in principle, was equally outraged by the German treatment of Belgium. In the circumstances, however, imagining like most people that the war would soon be over, he felt that joining up was the only honourable course of action. Unlike Sassoon, he chose to take a commission and, thanks to the Harlech Golf Club secretary - who had quickly contacted the depot of the Royal Welch Fusiliers with a mention of Graves's Officer Training Corps experience and family military background - Robert reported to the Fusiliers' regimental Headquarters in Wrexham just over a week after war was declared on 4 August 1914.

The depot was commanded by Lieutenant Colonel A. Hay and it was here that the Regiment reminded Graves that he had been given the enormous privilege of being commissioned a Special Reserve officer - admittedly a very lowly status, but nevertheless second only to that of a commissioned officer in one of the two regular battalions. Not for him he was told, 'the inferior New Army commission', but a permanent commission in the Royal Welch's Special Reserve Battalion.

When war is declared, belligerent nations close all borders. Enemy citizens are immediately interned, and the summer of 1914 found visitors from both Britain and Germany on the wrong side of the frontiers. (Some, such as the poet Charles Hamilton Sorley on holiday in the Rhineland, managed to elude the advancing German army. Arriving in Belgium, Sorley was fortunate to reach England without being interned.) London and the provinces had more than 66,000 residents and visitors of German and Austrian nationality, waiters, sailors and salesmen, for example, who were caught by the war and quickly arrested as enemy aliens. Accommodation of all kinds was hastily commandeered for them and Graves was ordered from Wrexham to Lancaster, where a former engineering works now housed some 3,000 prisoners, including a number of children. The camp commandant was a lieutenant-colonel in the East Lancashire Regiment.

At first Graves seemed to enjoy his posting; he had a good relationship with his colonel, but he had constant worries from Royal Welch reservists under his command who were continually absenting themselves from the unit without leave. An unlucky accident marked his time at Lancaster - a powerful electric shock, possibly due to a lightning strike, during a routine telephone call from Western Command Headquarters in Chester about the victualling of a batch of internees from that area. For some years afterwards he was never quite

⁴ *The Assault Heroic*, R.P. Graves.

at ease when using the telephone - the after-effects of the incident probably also became part of his general nervous state after the war. He was soon recalled to the 3rd Battalion at Wrexham and in October he resumed his military training at the regimental depot there.

Casualties in the Royal Welch's regular battalions, especially in the ranks of the 1st Battalion, meant that Graves's contemporaries were constantly departing for France while he, equally anxious to go, was being held back at the depot - possibly because he had offended the adjutant, perhaps because he was not a conforming, neat and organised soldier and did not always get on easily with his fellow-officers. The Member of Parliament for Kilmarnock Burghs, Lt.W.G.C. Gladstone, for example, a 29-year-old grandson of the former Prime Minister and described by a friend as 'no soldier', had only recently been sent to France as a reinforcement to the 1st Battalion (later killed in action 13th April 1915), while Graves, a much younger man, was held back despite his keenness to go.

Although in *Goodbye to All That* Graves indicates that he was reported as scruffy, a nuisance and unsoldierly, he had enthusiastically adopted the regimental honour and cause as his own, and felt great pride in it. Somehow he began to show improvement and even received promotion to Lieutenant. Ironically it was a school accomplishment that caught the eye of the depot adjutant, Captain C. H. R.Crawshay (known as 'Tibs'), when his prowess in a regimental boxing bout won approval and his eventual listing for overseas service.

Robert Graves left the 3rd Battalion at Wrexham on 12 May 1915, on his way to France and the base camp at Le Havre. The other members of the draft were Jones-Bateman, recently a schoolboy at Rugby whose nickname was 'silent knight', Hanmer Jones, Robertson, McLennan and Watkin, with the addition five days later of other ranks from the Royal Welch. Much to their disappointment (Graves writes 'disgusted') they were being sent as officer reinforcements not for their own regiment but for the 2nd Welch Regiment, occupying a quiet sector in the mining village of Labourse, south of Béthune.

In 1758 the 2nd Welch had been numbered the 24th of Foot but later in that year it was redesignated the 69th Foot, eventually to be known in the army as 'the ups and downs' (because the number reads the same both ways up). Although not as senior in service as the Royal Welch, the Regiment and its battalions never the less had a very distinguished service record, which they set out in their Regimental History. (The Regimental History took exception to Graves's remarks in *Goodbye to All That* about the 2nd Welch battalion. His reference to its 'peaceful

Lieutenant W.G.C. Gladstone, MP. A week after being promoted to Lieutenant, Gladstone, who had been at the Regimental depot with Graves, was killed in action on 13 April 1915 whilst serving with the 1st RWF in the front line trenches at Laventie.

attitude', and a dozen lines of comment, were published with complaints at what he had written. Perhaps more by accident than design, the author, a Major-General, gives Graves the rank of Second Lieutenant when referring to his time with the Welch, although he was by then a full Lieutenant.)

One of Graves's more or less accurate anecdotes did nothing to honour the image of the 2nd Welch. Perceiving that a reference to murder would add to the potential popularity of *Goodbye to All That*, he found a genuine episode to suit his requirements: two soldiers of the 2nd Welch murdered their Sergeant-Major, although not when Graves was serving with the battalion in May 1915, the time indicated in the book: a lance-corporal and a private soldier had shot Company Sergeant Major Hayes the previous January during a drunken spree, and were later court-martialled and condemned to death by firing squad.

The 2nd Welch had taken part in the débâcle and failed attack at Aubers Ridge on 9 May 1915, suffering 256 casualties, of which eleven were officers - hence the need for the Royal Welch draft. Afterwards they were sent to re-group in the luxury of some quiet sector trenches previously held by the French. The Welch described the dugouts as 'almost works of art', some of them strengthened with steel girders. This rest period was soon over, however, for three days after Graves's arrival the whole battalion moved off to the dreaded Cuinchy sector. Its notorious brickstacks created an area of mining, bombing and mortar activity and it was here that Graves's fellow Royal Welch officer, Lieutenant Watkin, was wounded.

In *Goodbye to All That*, Graves describes the great brickstacks, where the Germans were very close. Each army held half of the stacks and,

The Brickstacks, Cuinchy. Taken from the position of the British front line in 1915, this modern photograph shows the area of the battlefield known as 'The Brickstacks'. Robert Graves was here in 1915 with the 2nd Welch Regiment and then later with the 2nd Royal Welch Fusiliers where his company occupied the canal-bank frontage. The village of Cuinchy lies to the left of the picture.

LA BASSEE CANAL

LA BASSEE CANAL

Vermelles, 1914 - as it looked when recaptured by the French in October 1914. Robert Graves was here in 1915, on attachment to the 2nd Welch Regiment. He saw the town square full of Royal Field Artillery guns.

> *Each side snipes down from the top of its brick-stacks into the other's trenches. This is also a great place for rifle-grenades and trench-mortars.*

There was constant fear on both sides of the front line of being blown up because of the constant mining and counter-mining activity taking place in the sector. Often the miners below ground were within earshot of each other, both sides hastily digging in their respective tunnels, each team hoping to be the first to complete and explode their mine. Not a pleasant region to serve in. Graves, who had many Welsh miners around him, describes a conversation between two recruits from the coal-fields, about the different seams of coals in Wales running from pit to pit across the counties, as 'one of the most informative conversations I ever heard'.

Late in June 1915 the 2nd Welch were sent to the Vermelles area, to begin training for the forthcoming Battle of Loos. Despite the area's reputation as 'a quiet sector', it was here that they suffered an 'orgy of shelling'. At Battalion Headquarters, for example, 32 shells and three bombs landed in their immediate vicinity in three consecutive days. A Royal Field Artillery battery occupied the town square in Vermelles and Graves took the opportunity of their presence to receive Holy Communion from the padre taking the service there.

Eighty-five years later, the town square in Vermelles.

Towards the end of July the Royal Welch Fusiliers reclaimed their officers. Of the five who had been with Graves in the 2nd Welch only

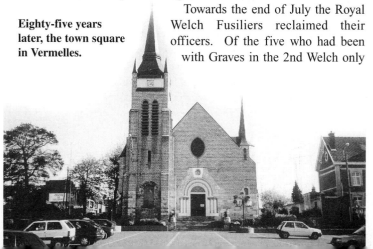

The church square at Laventie. Graves reported to the 2nd RWF in Laventie High Street in the summer of 1915, after his period with the 2nd Welch Regiment. Although many houses survived destruction, the church had been badly damaged by shellfire.

three were now available - Watkin had been wounded and McLennan had been sent home sick. Hanmer Jones and Jones-Bateman departed for the 1st Royal Welch, now desperate for reinforcements after their part in the Battle of Festubert on 16 May where, out of a total of 831 officers and men engaged, only six officers and 247 other ranks were left two days later. The dead included the Commanding Officer, Lieutenant Colonel Richard Gabbett and the Battalion adjutant. The Medical Officer, Lieutenant Kelsey Fry, who was later to serve with Graves and Sassoon, was amongst the wounded. The Corps advance gained just 600 yards but Captain Stockwell (later to command the battalion) and his Royal Welch party went forward about three-quarters of a mile.

Robertson and Graves made their deliberately leisurely way to Laventie to report to the 2nd Royal Welch. Despite some of his less than complimentary remarks about his time with the 2nd Welch, Graves later recognised that he had received an excellent training with them which prepared him for what was to come. He was fortunate that the 'peaceful attitude' of the 2nd Welch and the 'quiet' sectors in which they served had provided time for the Battalion to tutor him in the art of trench warfare. As he arrived at their Battalion Headquarters in Laventie High Street he was about to experience a less than peaceful attitude with his new battalion, the 2nd Royal Welch Fusiliers

Chapter Three

LIFE WITH THE RWF

Graves reached Laventie, a village about seven miles south west of Armentières, towards the end of July 1915 after some three months of active service with the 2nd Welch. If he had been expecting a welcome he was to be disappointed. At this time the 2nd Royal Welch were still operating as General Headquarters Troops and, unlike so many other regular battalions who had seen their officers and men melt away in battle, were still able to operate on a more or less peacetime basis; there had been casualties, of course, but mercifully these had been light. Regimental traditions and some peacetime regimental customs (even including parading in the summer uniform of shorts) echoed normal custom and a degree of snobbery, and Graves reported into an apparently unwelcoming atmosphere.

The Royal Welch Officers' Mess was in a château near Laventie church. It was here amongst his fellow officers that Graves felt unwelcome and less than popular during the few months of his stay with the battalion.

According to his autobiography, some unpleasantness began almost as soon as he arrived. Embarrassingly, he was accused of being improperly dressed and ordered to see the regimental tailor. Conforming to the custom in the 2nd Welch, Graves had appeared with his badges of rank as a lieutenant on the epaulettes of his uniform jacket. In previous months the 2nd Welch had taken part in some disastrous fighting in which officer casualties had been extremely high, a factor attributed to the prominence of their rank badges displayed on each of the tunic sleeves. Accordingly, they were moved to a less conspicuous position on each shoulder and therefore not so obvious to snipers. The 2nd Royal Welch, having had fewer casualties, obviously had not felt the need for such a change and continued with the peacetime custom of showing officer rank on the tunic cuffs. (In the Somme battle of 1916 some regimental officers wore the uniform of a private soldier in action, together with appropriate webbing equipment. Rank badges were worn on the epaulettes. When taking part in an attack some officers would carry a rifle so as to be indistinguishable from the men they were leading.)

Several other factors contributed to Graves's cool reception, not least of which was his lesser status in holding a temporary commission amongst so many who held a permanent one. His apparently rapid promotion to full lieutenant was not well received by those junior to him who, despite considerable service with the regiment, had still not achieved that rank. It also seems that the Battalion regarded temporary officers sent to them as being 'on approval' and there for continuous testing. Graves's own person style did not help, for he was inclined to give free rein to a somewhat abrasive or argumentative manner. He forfeited some acceptance by the regiment when a long serving sergeant and a Company Sergeant Major were reported by him for a breach of discipline which the colonel quickly decided it wise to disregard; and there was a more domestic occasion in Cambrin shortly after the Loos battle, when Graves clumsily trod on one of two kittens regarded as Battalion pets - but this came as the culmination of a series of apparent failures to adjust to the Battalion's way of

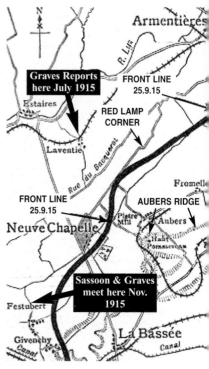

The Laventie sector. Graves used Red Lamp Corner as a landmark while patrolling in No Man's Land. Aubers Ridge was the scene of the 2nd Welch's disastrous attack on 9 May 1915, in which they suffered heavy casualties.

life. There was no criticism of his conduct in action, which was considered exemplary, but his failure to hit it off with other officers eventually led Lieutenant-Colonel Williams to arrange for him to be transferred to the 1st Royal Welch. In the meantime Graves was soon to go into action.

FACT OR EMBELLISHED FACT?

Whatever the atmosphere that the young officer created around him at this time (he was less than a year away from his school desk), it certainly stood him in good stead when he came to write his 'memoirs' and could turn his experiences into humorous incidents. Graves seems to have invented the concept of 'black humour' long before the expression became known, using irony and often deliberately distorted version of facts to reveal the true nature of people and events, and to recount what would be ridiculous if it were not so dangerous.

As one of his biographers has pointed out, the passage in *Goodbye to All That* relating to May-June 1915 is unreliable in referring to letters, and so heavily rewritten for subsequent editions as to lose much of its value as contemporary evidence. The chapter was 'reconstituted' and when checked against battalion records can be shown to be inaccurate in factual detail: but the sharpness of the contrast between home and the front line, and news of the deaths of friends and relatives, created a sense of unreality and disorientation. Letters home mentioned unhappiness, anxiety and uncertainty, and no doubt these elements, added to the aftermath of his unhappiness at school and his highly intelligent but combative nature to make him a difficult subaltern to manage. (This was also when he heard that the younger boy on whom his idealistically platonic emotions had been fixed at Charterhouse was discovered to be far less morally blameless than he had believed, a disturbing moment.)

When Siegfried Sassoon came to depict Graves in his fictionalised Sherston 'memoirs', he described Graves vividly under the invented name of 'David Cromlech':

At his best I'd always found him an ideal companion, although his opinions were often disconcerting. But no one was worse than he was at hitting it off with officers who distrusted cleverness and disliked unreserved utterances. In fact he was a positive expert at putting people's backs up unintentionally. ... David certainly was deplorably untidy, and his absent-mindedness when off duty was another propensity which made him unpopular. Also, as I have already hinted, he wasn't good at being 'seen but not heard'. 'Far too fond of butting in with his opinion before he's been asked for it', was often his only reward for an intelligent suggestion.

It seemed to be common wartime practice for newly joined subalterns to be immediately initiated into conditions at the front. As was to happen later to Siegfried Sassoon and Edmund Blunden, Graves writes that he was at once warned for duty and then instructed to make a patrol into No Man's Land accompanied by a sergeant, an order which he immediately saw as being a test which he would be unwise to refuse.

The patrol was uneventful and Graves and the sergeant returned safely to the British lines some two hours later, having crawled to

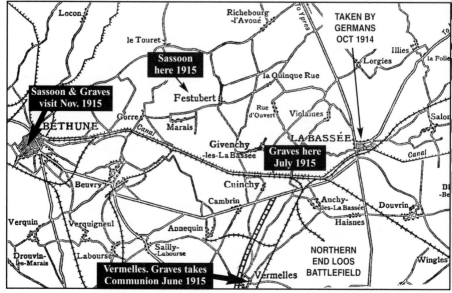

The battlefield area, where Graves and Sassoon served in 1915.

within a few yards of the German front line trenches. This patrol would not be his last; the 2nd Royal Welch placed great importance on maintaining their ascendancy over No Man's Land, and patrolling in front of the enemy trenches was one way to achieve this. Graves continued to play his part.

One of the Battalion officers, Sir Pyers Mostyn MC, was an enthusiast for this kind of patrol work, an eagerness he shared with fellow officer Second Lieutenant W.G. Fletcher. Fletcher's accurate knowledge of German frequently proved to be of tremendous help in their occasional encounters with enemy patrols: on one occasion Fletcher went out alone as far as the enemy's wire and recovered a French flag which the Germans had placed there – a very brave and widely respected soldier, Fletcher lost his life on duty in the front line, shot in the head by a sniper in March 1915. In due course the captured flag was sent to Eton College where he had been a master.[5] After Fletcher's death Mostyn continued with his forays into No Man's Land but on 7 August he was wounded in the arm whilst searching for an enemy listening post, and much to the Battalion's regret did not return to them after his recovery.

The Battalion was holding a sector facing east in front of Laventie near Fauquissart, their trenches stretching north-eastward as far as a point in the British front line called Red Lamp Corner which jutted out into No Man's Land just south of the village of Le Tilleloy. A red warning lamp was set at its furthest point in No Man's Land, as a

[5] W. G. Fletcher: before taking up his appointment at Eton, Fletcher taught at Shrewsbury School. His death inspired two of his colleagues there, Malcom White and Evelyn Southwell, to take commissions in the Rifle Brigade; both were killed in action in 1916, White on 1 July and Southwell in mid-September. This pair, who referred to each other as 'Man' and were together known as 'The Men', were commemorated in 1919 in a vivid and touching memoir, *Two Men*.

warning to avoid fire from the British front line penetrating this salient by accident - hence its name. Graves found it a useful marker when he patrolled in the area.

A long low hill-crest some 80 feet high, lying just under a mile in front of the British trenches, was Aubers Ridge, the objective of the disastrous attack by the British on 9 May 1915 in which the 2nd Welch had lost so heavily. The trenches were invariably waterlogged, as the original land drainage system, already inadequate, had been destroyed by shellfire. Across the battlefield, and almost parallel with the front line trenches, ran the natural barrier of the notorious Layes Brook. (In July 1916 the zone nearby was the scene of yet another failed attack by the British and Australians, culminating yet again in heavy casualties.)

Overall the distance between the front lines was about 400 yards - but at Red Lamp Corner the German front line was only some 80 yards away. The Royal Welch took the opportunity to construct a primitive bomb catapult which they also used from time to time to launch abusive messages to the enemy opposite.

It was vital for both sides that enemy patrols into No Man's Land could not approach unseen. The Royal Welch sent out working parties on several nights to cut down the long grass which was then encroaching on the battalion's outer defences, while the Germans opposite did exactly the same in front of their trenches. Although on these occasions it was normal for both sides to ignore each other and to carry on with the work in hand, on one occasion their customary unofficial arrangements were ignored and a Royal Welch in the working party was fired on and killed. On the following nights the German working parties were fired on in retaliation, bringing shouted obscenities from the German line.

Occasionally in war time there is a time for relaxation which may be private - writing letters, for example - or public, such as a concert. One officer serving with the Royal Welch, Lieutenant Dewhirst of the Loyals, was a professional actor who took part in one or two performances for the benefit of the troops out of the line. Enquiries by a general about the efficiency of newly joined subalterns brought a reply from the Commanding Officer of the 2nd Royal Welch, no doubt with Dewhirst in mind, that he understood that one of his subalterns had taken the part of the rear legs of a hippopotamus in a pre-war revue! On 14 August 1915 the Division ran an Athletics Meeting including a Horse Show. As would be expected at such a military event, speculation about the war and troop movements prospered and such gossip was, in general, disbelieved. However, one rumour proved to be

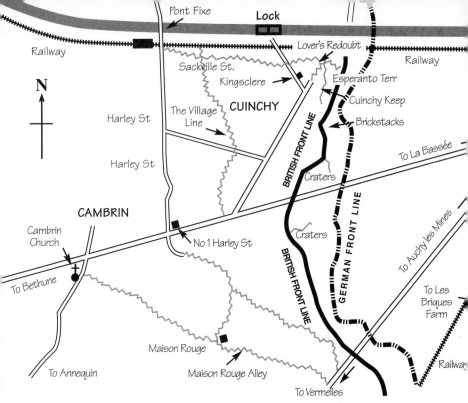

La Bassée Canal area south. Graves served in this area with both the 2nd Welch Regiment and the 2nd Royal Welch Fusiliers in 1915 and the northern end of the Loos battlefield on 25 September 1915. Edmund Blunden, later a friend of both Sassoon and Graves, served in this area in June-July 1916 and their war experiences here became the topic for long peace-time conversations.

of substance and three days later the 2nd Royal Welch were no longer Headquarters Troops but had marched to Béthune to become part of the 2nd Division under Major-General Horne, to take over some of the front from the French Army.

By 24 August the battalion was in the front line at Cuinchy near the notorious brickfield with its solid stacks of bricks, many about 18 feet in height and covering a base area of some 35 square feet. These formidable emplacements, in the sector where Graves had served when with the 2nd Welch earlier in the year, were mostly in German hands. His company was now allocated the trenches near the La Bassée canal and here, in a rat-infested dug-out built into one of the banks along the towpath, Graves made his home.

In addition to the 2nd Royal Welch, the 19th Brigade, of which the Battalion was now a part consisted of the 1st Scottish Rifles, 1st

Middlesex, 2nd Argyll & Sutherland Highlanders and 5th Scottish Rifles.

It was not long before Colonel Williams ordered a patrol to investigate a report that a German working party was taking advantage of the moonlit nights and operating on the Royal Welch's front. An understandably nervous Graves was detailed for this somewhat hazardous patrol, for the full moon made the battlefield scene as bright as day; but he was keen to go and crawled out into No Man's Land with his sergeant, making short rushes from crater to crater as opportunity arose and dropping into the sometimes unspeakable human debris to be found at the bottom. Miraculously unseen, they reached to within a few yards of a section of German soldiers lying in the grass and acting as a cover for the main working party nearby. After deciding not to shoot, Graves and his companion made their way back to the British lines and in doing so managed to escape an enemy machine-gun which opened fire on the British trenches.

It had been a nerve-racking experience, but there was more to be done. Giving the position of the German working party to a British field battery, a few minutes later Graves was gratified to hear the noise and shouts of the Germans as, with shrapnel bursting amongst them, they departed for the safety of their trenches. No doubt he considered that they had suffered a number of casualties. Writing in his autobiography Graves reported that he drew no praise for this dangerous exploit - on the contrary, he attracted some admonition for failing to fire at the Germans lying down in the grass.

The exploit in brilliant moonlight was a disturbing one and in his diary Robert's father Alfred notes his son's comment in a letter at the end of August about 'the dangerous clear light of an evil-looking moon'. (Although it makes no direct reference to the war, his poem 'I Hate the Moon' has the subtitle 'After a moonlight patrol near the Brickstacks'. It was written soon after this incident .)

Graves went on leave on 6 September, joining his family in North Wales. He found everything amazingly normal after his life at the front and enjoyed discussing poetry with his father - and the publication of extracts from his letters in The Spectator. It was a comforting and reassuring time before returning to his battalion some ten days later.

By now the 2nd Royal Welch was heavily involved with the preparations for the forthcoming Battle of Loos. As Graves and Sassoon's post-war friend, fellow-poet and memoirist Edmund Blunden was to discover with the Royal Sussex a year later, it was the Army's invariable practice to detail far too many men for any one task

Siegfried Sassoon with the Royal Welch Fusiliers. Officers of the 3rd Battalion, taken at the depot in June 1915. The Commanding Officer, Lieutenant-Colonel Jones Williams, is seated behind the shield and Sassoon is in the back row, ninth from the left. Some of his and Graves's friends are also present: Lt. Conning (back row, 1st left); 2nd Lt. David Thomas (back row, 4th from left); Lt. Stansfield (middle row, 4th from left); the two figures on the ground to the right of the shield are Lt. Orme (left) and 2nd Lt. Pritchard (right). COPYRIGHT ROYAL WELCH FUSILIERS MUSEUM.

- a pattern which often hindered the smooth completion of the numerous and exhausting tasks now allotted to the Royal Welch. The increased military activity in the British lines was not lost upon the Germans and the Battalion suffered some casualties from trench-mortars and the exploding of mines in addition to the usual rifle and machine-gun fire. Graves was back in the line with the Battalion a week before the Loos battle began.

The Loos battlefield stretched northwards from just north of Lens to Givenchy, located about a mile north of the La Bassée canal. As a site on which to fight a battle the whole area was far from ideal. A sector given over to coal mining, the landscape was thickly scattered with pit winding machinery and huge dumps of mining waste or slag heaps, quite unsuitable for the attacking British but a good defensive area for the defending Germans. The French General Joffre had chosen the position with his unfailing optimism, reluctantly supported by the British Secretary of State for War, Lord Kitchener.

There was a wider picture involved in the Allied decision to attack here. Firstly, the time had come for the British to take a more active role in the conduct of the war; and, secondly, it was obvious that any great success in this region would have an economic effect, going some

way towards helping to restore the industrial capacity of France, so much of which was in German hands. Furthermore, the British had brought some 5000 gas cylinders over to France, half of which were available for this front. It was hoped, therefore, that with a favourable wind the release of the chlorine gas would devastate the enemy and compensate for the obvious disadvantages of the battlefield.

The battle began at 6.30 am on 25 September 1915 along a seven mile front against very strong enemy resistance. Handicapped by a shortage of guns and ammunition and, very importantly, by the very moderate success of the gas weapon (because of a change in the wind direction), the full battle plan failed. Although success was nearly achieved at the southern end of the battlefield, the hoped-for breakthrough foundered through the exhaustion of the attacking troops and lack of reinforcements. The cost was heavy: while German casualties amounted to nearly 20,000, British casualties incurred in capturing about 8000 yards of enemy front came to some 60,000, including the lives of three generals. (The three were Major-Generals Sir T. Capper and G. H. Thesiger, both killed on 27 September, and F. D. V. Wing, on 2 October.)

Various actions continued, dying down on 13 October with the conclusion of fighting in the region of the notorious Hohenzollern Redoubt. Militarily, valuable lessons had been learned - although at a heavy cost in lives. Politically, however, the result was deemed unacceptable and a victim had to be found - so, in December, Sir John French was recalled to command Home Forces and General Haig (later, in January 1917, Field-Marshal) took over.

Graves's 2nd Royal Welch, part of 19th Brigade now transferred to the 2nd Division, held the trench lines at the north end of the battlefield in the region south of the La Bassée canal. For the troops of this division, 25 September was to bring heavy losses utterly devoid of success - a day of terrible misfortune.

The Brigade front line facing east was held by the 1st Middlesex,

45

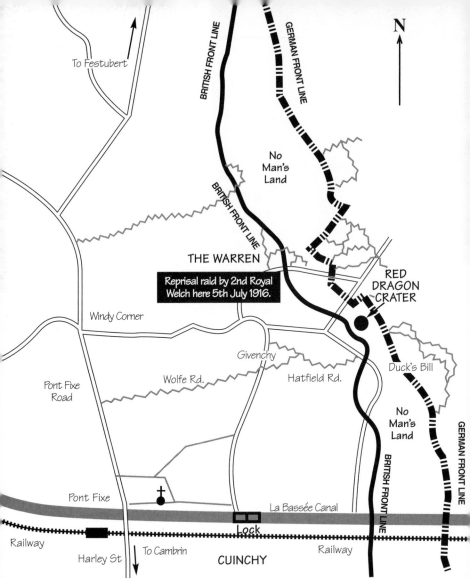

The Givenchy Sector. Note the Red Dragon Crater where German tunnellers exploded a mine under B Company, 2nd RWF, also The Warren where the battalion carried out its reprisal raid. The area was familiar to Graves through his service with the 2nd Welch and the 2nd RWF in 1915 and 1916.

with the 2nd Argyll & Sutherland Highlanders on their left and the 2nd Royal Welch in support. The intention was for B and C companies of the Royal Welch to reach the front line trenches just as the Middlesex had left. The 1st Scottish Rifles and 5th Scottish Rifles were held in reserve. The limited objectives appointed to the Brigade included the capture of the moated farm at Les Briques, near Auchy les Mines, and the railway line beyond between Haisnes and the canal area around La Bassée, a proposed advance of some 3000 yards. The objectives were limited because the 2nd Division's primary task was not to break through but to establish a flank on its left, facing north, to protect and cover the attacks of the divisions to their south.

Field-Marshal Earl Haig.

British artillery pounded the German front line trenches facing 19th Brigade front, but the troops holding it had long since departed for their support line from where they could easily open fire. Ten minutes before zero hour, No. 173 Tunnelling Company R.E. detonated two mines under the German front - thereby alerting the enemy that an attack was imminent. Moreover, the resulting craters were so large that the attacking British were forced to make their way through very narrow gaps between them, breaking up their formation and making excellent targets for the German soldiers.

Some time before 6.30 am the Special Accessory units of the Royal Engineers in the Middlesex and Argylls' trenches opened the valves on the gas cylinders, expecting the gas to drift towards the enemy lines -

Auchy-Les-Mines: The Battle of Loos. A modern view from the position of the front line trench, looking across No Man's Land, occupied by Robert Graves and the 2nd Royal Welch on 25 September 1915 during the Battle of Loos. The line of trees across the centre marks the track of a disused railway; beyond it, in the large clump of trees, lies Les Briques Farm near Auchy-les-Mines, one of the failed objectives of the battalion that day. The field in the foreground was strewn with the dead and wounded of the Argylls, Middlesex and Royal Welch as they attempted to go forward.

LES BRIQUES FARM

Les Briques Farm, Auchy-les-Mines, a recent photograph. This farm at the northern end of the Loos battlefield in September 1915 was allocated to the 2nd RWF for capture on the first day of the battle. They were unable to advance more than a few score yards and the farm remained in German hands.

but the wind was in the wrong direction and the chlorine gas drifted back into the British trenches. When it realised this, Brigade Headquarters sought permission to discontinue the release, but the order was not cancelled. Some of the Middlesex men climbed out of the front line trenches to avoid being gassed, as did the Argylls who made for nearby craters in No Man's Land. As the two battalions began their advance, many almost stifling in their rudimentary gas-masks, they encountered devastating German machine-gun fire deliberately aimed low, resulting in painful leg and ankle wounds. Many fell back into the trenches they had just left. Hardly any progress was made before the advance of both battalions was stopped within a few minutes, leaving the trenches and No Man's Land packed with dead and wounded men.

In a briefly successful effort, two Middlesex platoons, in particular the Grenade Reserves, made for an important crater position and actually captured it, hanging on until 1.15 pm when they were ordered to retire.

B and C Companies of the Royal Welch had made their way forward as instructed but, with the communication trenches full of wounded on their way to the rear Regimental Aid Posts, their progress to the front line trenches was slow. Once there the two companies climbed out of the trenches and into No Man's Land to go to the aid of the Middlesex. C Company managed about 40 yards, and B Company an even shorter distance, before the Royal Welch were mown down like their comrades before them. Lieutenant-Colonel Williams and his Second in Command, Major Clegg-Hill, were wounded: the adjutant, Captain C.S. Owen, took command of the Battalion. Men lying out in No Man's Land were ordered to dig for cover. No further instructions were

Maison Rouge, Cambrin. A series of communication trenches spread out in front of this building, such as Maison Rouge Alley which led to the British front line in September 1915 during the Battle of Loos. It was along one of these trenches that the 2nd RWF filed to support the 1st Middlesex in their attack in the battle.

received by either company until late in the afternoon when the Acting C.O. met one of the company officers who had crawled his way back to the British trenches - to be met, somewhat disturbingly, with the remark that the Acting C.O. thought that they were all dead. With that the survivors were instructed to begin the long crawl back to the trenches.

A Company, including Graves, and D Company made its way to the front line trenches, starting from Cambrin Church and making slow progress past the Maison Rouge and then down Maison Rouge Alley communication trench to the front line trenches and the support lines; but by then it was obviously suicidal for the two companies to go into the attack and the orders to go forward were cancelled.

Maison Rouge Alley, Battle of Loos. A recent view from the position of the British front line on 25 September 1915, showing the field through which Maison Rouge Alley Communication trench linked the rear areas near Maison Rouge with the forward trench, and down which Graves and his battalion made their way into battle on that day.

MAISON ROUGE

49

As soon as it was dark, parties went out into No Man's Land to bring in the wounded who had not been able to crawl back on their own. The discovery of two dead officers in the Middlesex with their bodies stripped of their uniforms gave rise to warnings about enemy impersonations. Amongst the hundreds of wounded passing through No. 1 Harley Street, Cambrin, behind the lines, where the 2nd Royal Welch's M.O. had his base, scores of men were suffering from the effects of gas. Few seem to have suffered severely, for the masks, though cumbersome to wear, were reasonably effective. Casualties amongst the 1st Middlesex numbered 455, while the 2nd Argylls suffered 330 officers and men killed, wounded and missing.

Although in theory both sides would go out to remove their dead from the battlefield, record their identity and then give them proper burial, this was seldom possible. On this occasion, however, two old soldiers in the Royal Welch, known 'characters', managed to go out during darkness and scour No Man's Land for souvenirs such as watches; their unauthorised absence was overlooked as they returned with their pockets full of identity discs taken from the dead. This enabled the various battalions to confirm to the next of kin with certainty that the soldier had been killed in action and was not merely 'missing'.

The 2nd Royal Welch had three officers and 34 other ranks killed and five officers and 71 men wounded, mainly in B and C companies, a total of 113 casualties. This was bad enough, but in the context of a Battalion at full strength with 200 men per company, not as devastating as has since been indicated - one comment, that the Battalion was 'decimated in a suicidal advance from Cambrin' is somewhat wide of the mark. Indeed, General Haking was still able to remark some six months later on the high proportion of the original regular soldiers who

Cuinchy Locks: taken from Pont Fixe, facing the German positions of 1915 where the bridge spans the canal. Somewhere beyond the lock on the canal bank, on the right, Robert Graves occupied his rat-infested dug-out in August 1915 when serving with the 2nd Royal Welch.

The Locks at Cuinchy. A modern view, taken from the canal towpath and looking towards the canal bridge, Pont Fixe. Graves was here in 1915 with the 2nd Welch and 2nd Royal Welch Fusiliers.

were still serving with the battalion.

In a letter to Edward Marsh in October 1915, referring to the 2nd Royal Welch's attack at Loos, Graves reports that it was designed in order to relieve the pressure on Loos and 'not with the object of breaking through'. Perhaps because of this, one writer describes the Battalion's attack as a 'decoy' whilst another calls it a 'diversion' - but in fact the opposite is true. The Official History (map, p.113) clearly indicates that the attack by the 2nd Division was a 'Main Attack' with 'limited objectives', an anticipated advance of almost two miles, bearing to the left, designed to give protected cover on the northern flank for those in action further south. In the same letter to Marsh Graves also wrote: 'Oh Eddie, there were some awful scenes that morning of the 25th!' and went on to describe his companions and their attitudes, education and personality in bitter terms.

On 27 September the Royal Welch were warned to be ready for another attack on the German lines, to be supported by the 5th Scottish Rifles. Graves would have been involved in this assault, but the orders were later cancelled; that afternoon, however, thirty men from the 1st Scottish Rifles under the command of Lieutenant F. Wayet were sent over into No Man's Land in broad daylight to carry out a bombing raid. Wayet actually reached the German lines but was killed in the close combat which followed. None of the patrol was ever seen again.

The next day the Royal Welch were close to the Hohenzollern Redoubt and expected to take part in an assault there, but once again, and to their satisfaction, they were not required. Since 25 September the weather had been unremittingly cold and damp and the Royal Welch, still in their summer uniform of shorts, felt the cold intensely, forcing many of the men to use sandbags for additional warmth. When the battalion relief arrived on 1 October the Royal Welch marched somewhat wearily to Sailly-Labourse. They were not sorry to leave the battlefield.

Two days later, a welcome clothing parade at Annezin allowed those wearing shorts and sandbag garments to replace them with new uniforms. There were several alarms from time to time as fighting took place in the region of Hohenzollern Redoubt with the Royal Welch standing-to but never being called to go forward. Finally, on 13 October, the British went on the attack trying to capture the Redoubt. They met with some success, taking its western portion and part of a position known as the Quarries some 1400 yards away to the south east. Among those killed that day, in an action at Hairpin Trench near the Quarries, was Charles Hamilton Sorley with the 7th Suffolks, a man who Graves in later years spoke of as 'one of the three poets of importance killed in the War'. (The others were Lieutenant Wilfred Owen of the 2nd Manchesters and Isaac Rosenberg, a private soldier with the 1st King's Own.)

Two days later Graves was promoted to the rank of captain. He was twenty years old.

VISIT NO. 1 - CAMBRIN and CUINCHY AREA

Leave the **A 26** motorway at Junction 6 and take the **N 41** to Cambrin. In Cambrin, turn right along the D 166 road and park near the church, on the left. It was here that Robert Graves entered the trenches on his way to the front line in 1915 on the Loos battlefield. The cemetery extension behind the church holds some 1,200 British graves, many of them grouped in battalions that were involved in the battles of Loos.

Return to the car, continue past the church to the traffic lights and turn right along the **N 41** again. At the next crossroads turn left into the Rue Anatole France, known to the British Army as Harley Street: the corner house on the right was where the M.O. of the 2nd Royal Welch Fusiliers had his Aid Post. At the far end of the street, just before the bridge over the canal, take a sharp turn to the right so that the La Bassée canal and the railway are on your left. It was here by the canal that Robert Graves sheltered in his rat-infested dug-out.

At the T-junction turn right, then after about 500 yards at a T junction turn right (Rue Basly). A hundred yards along it turn sharp left into the Rue Camille Desmoulins; this takes you through the area known as the Brickstacks (visible on the left) to the **N 41**. Turn right on the main road and go up to the next crossroads, of minor roads; turn left here (Rue Emile Zola) and proceed to the isolated farm house about half a mile along, on the right-hand side of the lane. It was from here, known to Robert Graves and his men as 'Maison Rouge', that the communication trenches led to the front line, across the fields towards the clearly visible spoil heaps.

Reverse direction, return to the crossroads; turning left on to the **N 41** and at the next crossroads turn right into Harley Street again. Repeat your route up the street to the railway station on the left, but this time go straight ahead across the canal bridge, familiar to the British as Pont Fixe, and turn right immediately beyond it. This takes you down the road past the canal lock buildings; follow the road on round to the left, to a junction beside a prominent modern spire. Turn right here and continue to the prominent divisional memorial to the West Lancashires, at the corner of the **D167**. Red Dragon Crater (the scene of Major Stanway's action) was in the field on the right near the road beyond the monument. Robert Graves was in action near here, on the left of the road, in the front line with the Royal Welch in June 1916 before he left for the Somme battlefield.

Turn and retrace your route, leaving the modern spire on your left and then turn right on to the **D 166** Cuinchy - Festubert road. Follow this into Festubert and turn right on to the D 72 by the church (this point was known to the British as 'Brewery Corner'). Sassoon and Graves served in this area when they joined the 1st Royal Welch in November 1915. Carry on to the busy D 947, turn left. Continue past the Portuguese Cemetery and then with the Indian memorial on the left, turn right on to the D 171. Go through Neuve Chapelle, with Fauquissart Military Cemetery on the left; at the next crossroads turn left on to the D 173, leading to Laventie where Graves joined the 2nd Royal Welch in July 1915. The mess was in a château by the church.

Leave Laventie on the **D 174E**; at the T-junction turn left on to the D 169 and almost immediately turn right and continue along it to the D 171. Turn left here and at the crossroads turn right along the D 175 (Rue Delva) to V.C.Corner Australian Cemetery. Park the car here; look half right across the fields to see the area where Graves and his battalion held the line in the summer of 1915.

It is worth visiting the Fromelles memorial park just beyond the cemetery, to view a newly-cleared area with bunkers and a striking modern statue of an Australian soldier rescuing a comrade.

For the quickest way back to the **A 26** from here, rejoin the D 171 through Neuve Chapelle to the junction with the D 947. Go across, past the Indian memorial (well worth a visit) and continue through Essars following signs round Béthune to rejoin the A 26 motorway at Junction 6.

The fighting died down after this, and the Battle of Loos and subsequent actions ended officially on 19 October 1915 – a battle started with such high hopes of success so nearly achieved, ending with heavy casualties, some ground gained and lessons learned.

After action in the Loos battle the 1st Royal Welch had successfully reached the outskirts of Cité St. Elie, a position about a mile south of Haisnes. Unfortunately no reinforcements arrived and the Battalion had to fall back. During their week on the battlefield their casualties were thirteen officers and 307 other ranks, including among the wounded Lieutenant Jones-Bateman, one of the officers who travelled with Graves to join the 2nd Welch Regiment earlier in the year.

Drafts would soon arrive to make up the deficit, including Graves in his new rank of captain; in the meantime, 'got rid of' by the C.O. of the 2nd Royal Welch, he was spending a pleasant month attached to the Brigade Engineers. His nerves had been affected by five months of front line duty and he would have welcomed a transfer home to training duties, but in November 1915 he was sent to join the 1st Royal Welch at Locon, north of Béthune.

Once commissioned, on 28 May 1915 Sassoon reported not, as would be expected, to the Regimental Depot at Wrexham but to a new hutted camp at Litherland, near Liverpool.

Litherland Camp, Liverpool, The parade ground in 1915, with the 3rd Royal Welch, and a similar view today.

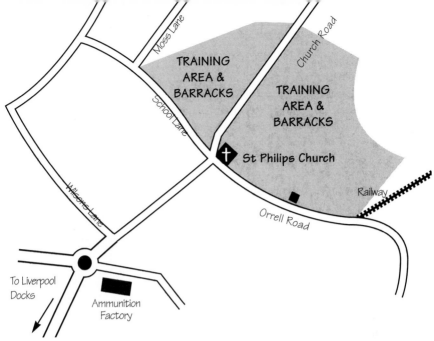

Litherland Camp. The site of the camp has been completely redeveloped and the roads realigned - the narrow lane that ran through the camp is now a dual carriageway, Church Road. An anti-aircraft battery was located near Wilson's Lane to deal with Zeppelin raids on the nearby docks. Contrary to local belief, Liverpool was not reached by Zeppelins although raiders did drop bombs on Bolton, not far away, in September 1916.

LITHERLAND CAMP

With the rapid expansion of the Army - by the end of 1914 over a million men had enlisted - it was soon realised that barracks accommodation in the UK was totally inadequate, even when former married quarters were taken over. Plans were immediately put in hand for hutted camps to be built throughout the United Kingdom, and within a year accommodation was available for some 850,000 men. Two of these built under the scheme were to become well known to Graves and Sassoon - the camp at Litherland, today unrecognisable as part of a housing estate, and a larger camp at Kinmel Park near Rhyl in North Wales, parts of which are still used by the British Army.

Sassoon's officer training began straight away, and there was much to learn. Part of the course took him to Pembroke College, Cambridge where he shared a room with his young friend Second Lieutenant David Thomas (depicted vividly and affectionately as 'Dick Tiltwood' in *Memoirs of an Infantry Officer*), a Sandhurst graduate.

Back in camp in mid-August, Sassoon's instruction continued for another two months until, now fully trained, he was given draft leave before departing to France to join the 1st Royal Welch holding the line near Festubert

In November the war came sharply close to home with news of the death of his younger brother, 27-year-old Second Lieutenant Hamo Sassoon, who had come over from South America on the outbreak of war to join the Royal Engineers. Wounded at Gallipoli, he died on 1st November and was buried at sea. Sassoon's poem 'To My Brother', written in mid-December 1915, mourns the loss and looks to the memory of his brother to lead him forward. There is no trace in it of the irony, anger and real despair which was soon to appear in his poetry.

2nd Lieutenant David Thomas. Sassoon's 'Dick Tiltwood'

Festubert. In ruins in 1915 when Sassoon went through the village to the front lines nearby, it was later completely rebuilt. A view from Brown's Road Military Cemetery.

Suvla Bay. Sassoon's brother Hamo was wounded here on 28 October 1915 and died of his wounds three days later. He was buried at sea.

SECOND LIEUTENANT HAMO WATTS SASSOON

Hamo Sassoon was born 4th August 1888 and, like his elder brother Siegfried, was educated at Marlborough College. When war was declared he was working in the Argentine for a prominent engineering firm, Walker & Co., and, like many British subjects working overseas at the time, returned to England to enlist. By 16 June 1915 he had been given a commission in the Royal Engineers and left for Gallipoli a month later. On 28 October he was at Suvla Bay. Going out into No Man's Land following a British attack, to supervise the construction of some new barbed wire entanglements, he was very badly wounded in the leg. Not wishing to disclose the position of his men to the Turks, he deliberately avoided making any noise and crawled back to the British trenches. Although he made light of his injury, he was taken to the Field Ambulance where the Medical Officer diagnosed a serious wound which would necessitate amputation, his condition aggravated by the crawl back to the trenches. From the Casualty Clearing Station Hamo was taken aboard the hospital ship SS Kildonan Castle where he died on 1 November. He was later buried at sea; his name is on the panels of the Helles Memorial.

Hamo Sassoon.

Matfield War Memorial. The village memorial, near the Sassoon family home Weirleigh, Kent, records the name of Hamo Sassoon.

This distressing news naturally had an impact on Sassoon, but it affected his mother particularly deeply. Turning to spiritualism for consolation, like so many others, she waited for Hamo's spirit to come to her and, in desperate belief in his eventual return, she always kept his room ready for him. Her spiritualism led to an incident with Robert Graves in 1917 that was to enrage Sassoon more than a decade later. (Graves's family had also suffered: a cousin, Major C. G. M. Blomfield, was killed in action with the Royal Warwickshires in the Ypres Salient in June 1915 and another cousin, Cecil Graves, was wounded and taken prisoner with the 1st Royal Scots Fusiliers in September 1914. Fleet Paymaster Cooper, another relative, was lost at sea when the cruiser HMS *Monmouth* went down with all hands, sunk by Admiral von Spee's squadron off Coronel in November 1914.)

Major C. G. M. Blomfield. A cousin of Robert Graves, killed in action on 9 June 1915.

After a few days at the notorious Etaples Infantry Base Depot, Sassoon and David Thomas reported to the Battalion at Béthune on 24 November 1915, within easy reach of the front line near Festubert. The 1st Royal Welch was to be their home for the next few months. The Commanding Officer was Lieutenant-Colonel J.R.M. Minshull Ford, a regular officer who had served as a captain

HMS *Monmouth*. Fleet-Paymaster John Cooper RN, a relative of Robert Graves, was lost when the ship was sunk with all hands by von Spee's Naval squadron on 1 November 1914. *Inset:* Admiral von Spee.

in 1914 with one of the Territorial Force battalions. It was well known in the 1st Royal Welch at the time that Minshull Ford was expecting rapid promotion to the rank of Brigadier-General and two months later, following a divisional re-organisation, he took command of 91st Brigade in the 7th Division.

Sassoon was to remain among friends, for David Thomas and Second Lieutenant N.Stansfield (who had been with him at Litherland) were both sent to C Company with him. The company was under the benevolent command of Captain E.J. Greaves (Sassoon's fictional 'Barton') whose brother Ralph was serving with the Royal Welch as a Lieutenant with the 2nd Battalion. Others in C Company were Second Lieutenants Edmund Orme ('Ormand') and Julian Dadd ('Durley'). Julian Dadd's brother, Lieutenant Edmund Dadd, commanded A Company. The family shared the Sassoons' cause for family grief, for their brother Leading Seaman Stephen Dadd, a gifted sculptor serving with the Anson battalion of the Royal Naval Division, had been killed in action early on the morning of 5 July 1915 in a skirmish with some Turkish troops who had penetrated the Battalion's trenches.

No time was lost in introducing Sassoon to trench life at Festubert, a ruined village about three miles south west of Neuve Chapelle. The day after reporting, he joined a Battalion working party of 60 men; after travelling by narrow gauge railway up to the rear area, for a further two hours he and his men struggled another 3/4 mile to the front line trenches. As the ground here was marshy and unsuitable for trench-digging, breastworks - sometimes called 'grouse butts' - were built for protection, labour that kept the working party fully occupied

A march past at Festubert. Taken in 1915 about a mile behind the front lines; British troops march past the saluting base where General Joffre, Generalissimo of the armies in the western theatre of war, and Field-Marshal Sir John French take the salute.

Leading Seaman Stephen Gabriel Dadd, killed in action at Gallipoli with the Anson Battalion of the Royal Naval Division. His two brothers Edmund and Julian served with Sassoon and Graves with the 1st RWF in the Bois Français trenches.

until late that night. After a day's rest Sassoon took charge of another party working near the front line on a frosty moonlit night, finally getting back to billets in the early hours of the next day. What he described as his 'first front-line poem', 'The Redeemer', was inspired by these working-parties, with the not-unusual theme of the British soldier as a Christ-figure.

It was here that Robert Graves and Siegfried Sassoon first met, the start of a long but far from straightforward friendship. In *Goodbye to All That* Graves described how he found a book in a Company mess that was 'neither a military text-book nor a rubbishy novel', noted the owner's name written inside it, and immediately sought him out. Despite the great differences in personality their shared interest in poetry created an instant *rapport*, and the next day they both went off to nearby Béthune for tea. Sassoon found Graves to be 'an interesting creature'. He also remarks that Graves was 'very much disliked' – and as Sassoon had only been with the 1st Royal Welch for four days the comment suggests that Graves's abrasive manner and reputation was already known in the Battalion before Graves joined them.

Both men recorded their delight at discovering a congenial companion in a setting where literary leanings were generally non-existent; Graves, the younger by several years, was quick to point out the inappropriateness of Sassoon's style to their present circumstances, and Sassoon responded promptly; the plunge into what came to be recognised as his characteristic war poetry was quickly accomplished, with his hard-earned technical skills proving their worth as he gave expression to his new experiences.

A POETIC STYLE FOR WAR-TIME

The poem that initially inspired this guidance from Graves was Sassoon's 'To Victory', which opens 'Return to greet me, colours that were my joy,/Not in the woeful crimson of men slain, ...' and ends 'Come from the sea with breadth of approaching brightness,/When the blithe wind laughs on the hills with uplifted voice.' Sassoon had already commented on draft poems that Graves had shown him, saying that they 'were too realistic'; but, as Graves responded ('in my old-soldier manner'), this was before Sassoon had been in the trenches and 'he would soon change his style'. Graves's own war poems varied between brutal description, such as in 'A Dead Boche' or 'Goliath and David', and imaginative but menacing images ('Hate Not, Fear Not' or 'The Patchwork Quilt').

In some senses, Graves did for Sassoon what both men were later to do for Wilfred Owen - urging the absolute necessity of writing about 'what you know' and of moving beyond the more romantic and lyrical flights of peace-time language.

By nightfall, and again for the following day, Sassoon was back in the front line area supervising working parties until the Battalion moved out on rest to billets in Gonnehem.

With General Sir Douglas Haig taking over from Sir John French in mid December 1915, this was a good time for the Allies to assess their situation. There were many problems: the year had not been a good one for the British, the struggle at Neuve Chapelle had cost the British nearly 600 officers and some 12,000 men to gain an advance of around 3000 yards. (The casualties included Sassoon's cousin, a 36-year-old gunner officer, Lieutenant Norman Donaldson who was killed in action on the 10th March 1915. He has no known grave and is commemorated on the Le Touret Memorial, just over a mile north of Festubert.)

The battles at Aubers Ridge, Festubert and Loos had taken a heavy toll, not least on the battalions of the Royal Welch Fusiliers. A new and

British Gas Mask 1915. A 'trench helmet' of the type issued to the 2nd RWF before the Battle of Loos. Instructions directed that during the advance the helmet, which Graves calls 'a tube-helmet', should be worn rolled up on the head. This explains why wounded soldiers photographed after the battle appear to be wearing woollen hats with glass eye-pieces.

more lethal poison gas now appeared: on the day that Haig took over command of the British Expeditionary Force, phosgene was released by the Germans for the first time, in the Ypres Salient. The end-of-year assessment showed that total casualties on the British side since the hostilities began numbered over half a million. The French had suffered even more terribly with a total of nearly two million - from a total national population smaller than that of Great Britain - of which the huge figure of one million were killed or missing.

Understandably concerned at their casualty list, the French urged early offensive action on the part of their British allies in order to wear down the enemy. It was eventually proposed that, together with other military commitments, the British should take the offensive on a front of about 20,000 yards in the Somme area in the summer of 1916. As good (and junior) allies, the British could not oppose the project; the appropriate orders were given which would eventually engulf further enormous numbers, including both Sassoon and Graves, at that time respectively serving with the 1st and 2nd Royal Welch.

Meanwhile the 1st Royal Welch were under orders. By 5 December 1915 the battalion had left Festubert for a railway journey from Lillers to a training area near the village of Saleux, south of Amiens. It was the first move in their journey towards the trenches and the carnage of the Somme battlefield.

Graves had left the battalion on 14 January 1916 to attend as an instructor at the Base Camp at Harfleur, and was to be away some two months. When the the Transport Officer, Lieutenant R. Ormrod, went on leave shortly afterwards, Sassoon - with his skill and knowledge of the ways of horses - was a natural choice to take temporary charge. Soon, however, word came through that Ormrod had been retained in England and would not be coming back to the Battalion, and Sassoon's appointment became semi-permanent. There was time for enjoyment as well as work and training, and Sassoon found pleasure in exercising various chargers from the transport lines. There was time, too, for a

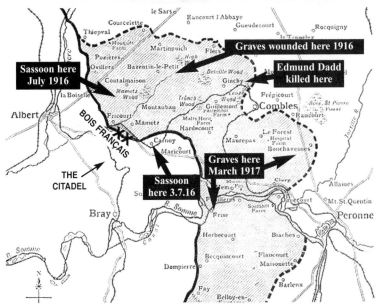

The Somme Battlefield. The dotted line shows the point reached by the Allies on 18 September 1916. Sassoon's poem 'At Carnoy' describes a scene on 3 July, just before the 1st RWF moved up to attack Mametz Wood.

visit to Amiens and its impressive cathedral one Sunday, a train journey of about 18 miles. By the end of January, however, the Battalion was on the move to the new British front line near Fricourt, passing the elegant château at Querrieu (soon to be General Rawlinson's Fourth Army Headquarters) and then stopping overnight at Pont Noyelles nearby, just across the River Hallue. By the evening of 1 February the 1st Royal Welch, now nearly 1000 strong, were at Morlancourt and the next day went into the line at Bois Français, hitherto held by the French, about three miles east of the town of Albert.[6]

The next day Minshull Ford's ambition for promotion was satisfied; promoted to Brigadier-General, he left the battalion to

General Rawlinson and Field Marshal Haig on the steps of the Château at Querrieu, Rawlinson's Headquarters in 1916. The Fourth Army Transport Officer was a Royal Welch officer, enabling Sassoon and fellow officers of the regiment to obtain transport into Amiens.

63

[6] Bois Français trenches: the wood at the west of the front line contains the grave of H.Tomasin of the 26th Infantry Regiment French Army, who was killed in 1915.

take command of 91st Brigade, 7th Division. (In due course he became Major-General J.R.Minshull Ford CB, DSO, MC, and died in 1948.)

The 1st Royal Welch was one of the four battalions forming the 22nd Brigade which was also in the 7th Division. In addition to the Royal Welch, there was one other regular battalion, the 2nd Royal Warwicks. A New Army battalion, the 5th Manchester Pals (20th Manchesters) under the command of Lieutenant Colonel Harold Lewis, a 35-year-old former Indian Army officer (of the Baluch Horse), together with the 24th Manchesters, raised in the Lancashire town of Oldham and known as the Oldham Pals, completed the Brigade's infantry complement.

The Brigade front of about 500 yards occupied bare rolling ground on a chalk ridge facing the devastated village of Fricourt. Much of it consisted of a series of mine craters, for both the British and German tunnellers frequently exploded charges in the front line area. It was a harrowing business for the troops holding the trenches, for danger came not only from the unexpected enemy explosions but from the British side too. On one occasion, when the trenches were held by the Oldham Pals, they were told that a British mine would be set off sometime during their tenure of the trenches. No precise time or even place was given by the Tunnelling Company, so the troops spent a nerve-racking day manning the line in the expectation of the trenches being blown up at any moment. Fortunately, when the mine was eventually blown it erupted well under the enemy's lines.

Holding the high ground was seldom the good fortune of the British soldier and, pleased though the Brigade may have been at this more advantageous position, their pleasure was somewhat undermined by having the enemy trenches facing them along the same ridge, running in some cases within 40 yards of the British trench line.

A strong-point established at the rear of the trenches, Maple Redoubt, was to be held at all costs in the event of an enemy breakthrough, pending a counter attack from the support lines. It also accommodated Battalion HQ, the bombing platoon, medical officer and stretcher-bearers. As a tempting target for the Germans it often came under fire. On 6 February, for example, when the 1st Royal Welch were in support of the Oldham Pals who were holding it, the redoubt came under heavy fire on two consecutive days, killing one officer, the Regimental Sergeant Major, a Company Sergeant Major and 14 other ranks, and wounding one officer and eleven men. Beyond, and out of enemy sight but still within artillery range, an area of dugouts known as the Citadel lay about 1200 yards to the rear, close to the road up from Bray to Fricourt. It was possible to continue past the Citadel towards Fricourt - and as there was no barrier across the road, it was not unusual for motor-cycle despatch riders to find themselves in No Man's Land and forced to beat a hasty retreat under fire from the Germans in Fricourt village.

The new Commanding Officer was Lieutenant Colonel C.I. Stockwell, known unofficially as 'Buffalo Bill' and well recognised for his military efficiency. He had served with distinction with the Battalion as a captain, particularly at Festubert in May 1915, but the beginning of February 1916 saw him in the Ypres Salient acting as Brigade Major to Brigadier-General C.D. Shute's 59th Brigade. On 20 February the train in which Stockwell set out from Poperinghe railway station came under long-range shellfire and was even pursued by a German aircraft trying to drop bombs on the line. He was glad to get away.

During several changes of train on his way to the Battalion, Stockwell inadvertently dropped his wallet, which made for some financial embarrassment until a paper-shop proprietor advanced him 25 francs; but on reporting at the Battalion's Headquarters he was delighted to renew acquaintance with several of his former friends - in

Lieutenant-Colonel C.H.R. Crawshay (left) and Lieutenant-Colonel C.I. Stockwell. Two officers of the Royal Welch Fusiliers, photographed before the Great War, who later became battalion commanders. Both Graves and Sassoon served under both men.

Captain M.S.Richardson, 1st Royal Welch Fusiliers. Died of wounds, 19 March 1916. One of the three battalion officers killed within 24 hours of each other in the trenches at Bois Français, all friends of Graves and Sassoon (the others were David Thomas and David Pritchard). Gazetted into the 2nd Royal Welch in 1914, he was present at Ypres when the battalion was involved in the Christmas truce of 1914. Wounded in April 1915, he returned to France and joined the 1st Royal Welch; he was badly wounded in the front line on 18 March 1916 and died on his way to the Field Hospital next day.

particular the Medical Officer, Lieutenant W. Kelsey Fry M.C. who had now recovered from his wounds received at Festubert. By 22 February Stockwell had made his assessment of the front line, and had much to say about the poor condition of the trenches and their wire defences. The Oldham Pals were holding the line during Stockwell's visit when a sudden bombardment opened up and a false gas alarm was given by the Pals battalion. The 1st Royal Welch, in support, stood to arms ready for the expected attack.

Sassoon had just brought up the transport and was at the Citadel, ready to unload the battalion's rations, when the gunfire began - but it turned out to be a German raid on another part of the line and very soon everything returned to normal. He returned to the transport lines to be told by his good friend Lieutenant and Quartermaster Joe Cotterill that he was to go on leave the next day.

On 12 March 1916 Graves returned from his eight-week course, taking his turn in the front line. Meanwhile, whenever the Battalion was holding the trenches, working parties were out in No Man's Land continuing the never ending task to improve the battalion's defences, renovating the wire and filling sandbags.

It was whilst carrying out this type of work on the night of 18 March that David Thomas, Sassoon's much-loved friend, was wounded in the throat. Lieutenant Kelsey Fry, the Medical Officer who was a throat surgeon in civilian life, emphasised the need for absolute immobility; but as he moved to reach for a letter in his tunic pocket to hand it over for posting, Thomas began to choke, and even with his skill as a surgeon Kelsey Fry was unable to help. The young man was dead within a few minutes.

It was a disastrous night after a period of apparent immunity, for David Thomas was not the only casualty that night: Second Lieutenant David Pritchard, the Trench Mortar Officer, was killed near Maple Redoubt just after midnight and, after David Thomas was wounded, Captain M.S. Richardson went up to the line with Lance Corporal Chamberlain to check on the wiring party's work when a shell dropped near them, killing the officer and badly wounding Lance Corporal Chamberlain. The total casualties that Saturday/Sunday night now amounted to three officers and one non-commissioned officer.

Next day Sassoon learned of these sad deaths - his friend David Thomas and his two companions, Pritchard and Richardson. That night he and Graves were present in the cemetery as in the presence of the Brigade Chaplain the bodies, each wrapped in an army blanket, were slowly lowered into the ground.

The three officers are buried in the same row of graves at Point 110 New Military Cemetery just behind the lines. Lance-Corporal Chamberlain, who died at the Casualty Clearing Station, is buried in Corbie Communal Cemetery.

SASSOON, GRAVES AND THE DEATH OF FRIENDS

This series of unlucky deaths affected Sassoon and Graves very deeply, and both the events and the grief they caused are dealt with at length in their later writing. Sassoon, who was deeply devoted to David Thomas, was profoundly moved by this particular loss. His published diary records, under 19 March 1916, 'the evil news', his memories of peace-time friendship, his overwhelming grief; and also the burial of Thomas, Richardson and Pritchard in 'the half-clouded moonlight' with Robert Graves beside him, 'his white whimsical face twisted and grieving'. Here, as well as in his 'Sherston' memoirs and his poetry, the cheerful youthful companion is remembered and mourned in some of Sassoon's most emotional lines. His poems 'A Subaltern', 'The Last Meeting' and 'A Letter Home' all refer to David Thomas and, when he came to write the 'Sherston' memoirs years later, from his diaries, he refers to hearing of the deaths: 'No news could have been worse'.

Graves, for his part, had been very conscious of the way in which he, Sassoon and David Thomas had formed something of a threesome, going about a good deal together, enjoying endless talk and occasional bursts of football in their rest periods. In *Goodbye to All That* he gives a vivid description of the fateful night when the three officers were killed - coming, as he records, just after the adjutant's comment that the battalion had managed to remain remarkably unscathed.

He also remarks, a little later, how Thomas's

The grave of David Thomas at Point 110 New Military Cemetery, Fricourt. Both Robert Graves and Siegfried Sassoon were present at the burial

The graves of Captain Richardson and 2nd Lieutenant Pritchard at Point 110 New Military Cemetery, Fricourt. Both these officers were killed in action within a few hours of the death of David Thomas.

> death had contributed to a change in Sassoon's approach to the war, inspiring his almost desperate urge to take risks and out-do everyone else in his onslaughts on the enemy.
>
> Their fellow-officer in the Battalion, Bernard Adams, also went on to give a detailed account of these events in his war memoirs, *Nothing of Importance.*

Sassoon's time with the Battalion transport came to the end soon after this episode, and he went into the line with C Company. A week or two later Lieutenant W. E. Rowley from the St. Pancras Battalion of the London Regiment arrived to take over as Transport Officer.

Point 110 New Military Cemetery, Fricourt. David Thomas, Mervyn Richardson and David Pritchard are buried here in the same row just behind the cemetery wall. The trees on the horizon mark the Bois Français trench line of 1916.

BOIS FRANÇAIS

TRANSPORT OFFICER

The role of the Transport officer was an exacting one which included the welfare of all the horses and responsibility for the maintenance of the limbers, field cookers and various carts belonging to the battalion. It was his task to organise the movement of personnel and provisions. In addition Sassoon, an officer with little seniority or experience of the work, would have been in charge of some 60 men, many of them 'old soldiers' - the few survivors from the battles of 1914 and 1915. It was during Stockwell's inspection of the battalion transport that he implied, no doubt tactfully, that Sassoon was wasted as Transport Officer; and as Sassoon replied that he would like to rejoin C Company, his return to company duty quickly followed. A replacement sent out from England joined the battalion shortly afterwards.

A new type of gas mask now being distributed to the battalion depended for its efficiency on the wearer's ability to breathe through the nose, but Graves's nose was so damaged by his past boxing activities that he could not use the new respirator. Kelsey Fry advised an operation and Graves accordingly departed for England, arriving there on 27 March 1916. He was eventually away from France for ten weeks, for after the operation he went on leave followed by a period at the Regimental Depot at Litherland. Here he met Lieutenants Jones-Bateman and Watkin, with whom he had served in the 2nd Welch, both still recovering from wounds.

While he was away the 1st and 2nd Royal Welch were embroiled in the murderous Somme battle which began on 1 July 1916 and, according to Sassoon, Graves's chance absence in the comfort of the depot did not go unremarked in the ranks of both battalions.

Stockwell's insistence that the Royal Welch must consistently hold the initiative in No Man's Land involved patrolling both by night and by day, and Sassoon took part in these activities. On 10 April 1916 he went out into No Man's Land in bright moonlight with two bombers - Privates Leigh and Grainger – plus Acting Corporal Richard O'Brien, a very reliable NCO renowned for his patrolling ability, and a favourite of his. As they reached the end of the British wire they saw four Germans crawling towards them. The bombers threw some dozen grenades but the enemy soldiers managed to escape, despite Sassoon chasing after one of them. The Germans retaliated, and in the subsequent shelling of the Royal Welch front line a very well-regarded soldier (Private F. Shooter) was killed and two others wounded. As Brigade wanted to identify a dead soldier lying out in No Man's Land the patrol made a detour, only to discover that he was a long dead Frenchman. Nevertheless they brought in the man's boot – with his leg still inside! A similar patrol the next night with Private Leigh brought them right to the German wire. Everything was quiet and as nothing was to be seen, they both returned to the British lines. (Private Leigh was killed at Delville Wood on 30 August 1916.)

Towards the end of April Sassoon was sent to Fourth Army School at Flixécourt for a busy month's course.

This turned out to be a comfortable stay, and he enjoyed

Flixécourt. A modern view of the imposing building that was used by the 4th Army Infantry school in 1916. At Christmas that year the owners, Monsieur and Madame Pierre Saint, were presented with an engraved silver bowl from Officer Instructors, 4th Infantry School.

meeting a former pupil and Senior Prefect from Marlborough College (Sassoon's old school), a contemporary and friend of Charles Hamilton

Flixécourt; another imposing building, though now neglected. When visited by King George V in August 1918 it was in use as 4th Army Headquarters. It seems likely that it was also used by the 4th Army Infantry School in 1916 when Sassoon attended a course here.

Sorley. The officer, Marcus Goodall ('Allgood'), of the 1/5th York and Lancasters was clearly an efficient soldier for, although only 21 years old, he already held the rank of captain. His name was soon to be added to the growing list of Sassoon's friends who died in battle, however, for by 14 July 1916 he had suffered wounds received in his Battalion's recent action near Thiepval (Somme) and had died at the Casualty Clearing Station at Puchevillers.

During the course Sassoon attended one of the bloodthirsty lectures and accompanying demonstrations run by Major Campbell on the use of the bayonet, well remembered and remarked upon (with varying degrees of approval) by all who heard the Major. With his mind turning towards a more ironic treatment of the war, Sassoon wrote 'The Kiss' after this lecture. It opens 'To these I turn, in these I trust -/Brother Lead and Sister Steel./To his blind power I make appeal,/I guard her beauty clean from rust' and although a number of commentators, including Robert Graves, remarked that it appeared to be a

4th Army Officers School, Flixécourt, April 1916. Sassoon is sitting in the front row, third from the right. As the officer in the back row, standing fourth from the right (arrowed), appears to be wearing a York and Lancaster Regiment cap badge, this may well be Sassoon's Marlburian friend Marcus Goodall ('Allgood') who died of wounds on 14 July 1916. COURTESY IMPERIAL WAR MUSEUM.

Kiel Trench; a modern photograph, taken from the site of the British trenches at Bois Français, looking across No Man's Land towards the German front line and in particular at the line of tall trees; this was the site of Kiel Trench in 1916. It was here that Corporal O'Brien lost his life on 26 May that year; Sassoon's courage during the action won him the Military Cross.

straightforward celebration of death-dealing weaponry, he insisted throughout his life that it was intended as a satire on bayonet fighting, which he abhorred. Graves's interpretation and 'mis-reading' of the poem contributed to their later falling-out. 'The Kiss' is dated 25 April 1916, and it was only four days after this that his first trench poem, 'The Redeemer', achieved publication in *The Cambridge Magazine*.

By 22 May Sassoon was back with his Battalion. The same day brought changes in 22nd Brigade and, much to their surprise, the Oldham Pals changed places with a regular battalion, the 2nd Royal Irish Regiment, and took on a new role as a Pioneer battalion. Sassoon's animosity towards the Germans following David Thomas' death had still not abated and he was anxious to resume his personal vendetta against them as soon as he rejoined the Battalion. The perfect opportunity soon presented itself, for Brigade orders required an officer-led raiding party of 25 men including five NCOs, one of whom was O'Brien, to attack the German front line at Kiel Trench. Sassoon was bitterly disappointed that, despite his skills in such work, his friend Lieutenant Stansfield had been chosen to lead the raiders.

At 10.30 p.m. on 25 May, therefore, Stansfield's party formed up with blackened faces. As usual in raids of this kind, they were equipped for close-quarter fighting with the spade edges of entrenching tools sharpened, hatchets in their webbing belts, bombs, and knobkerries. Corporal O'Brien led the way boldly with a few others into the darkness of No Man's Land, laying a trail of lime to the German trenches for the rest of the party to follow. Sassoon took charge of an evacuating party which lay out some twenty-odd yards beyond the British trenches, ready to cover the return of the raiders.

The raid was a failure. The alarm was raised as they tried to negotiate the enemy barbed wire and the British party was involved in a bombing fight in which twelve of the raiders became casualties, in particular, Sassoon's Corporal O'Brien. Going out into No Man's Land, Sassoon met the wounded Lieutenant Stansfield being assisted back to the British lines by two of his men and learned that O'Brien was lying badly wounded at the bottom of a deep mine crater. Collecting some helpers from the British trenches, he managed to get a rope round the wounded NCO, who was brought to safety with the aid of a stretcher-bearer and other men. Under Sassoon's supervision all the remaining wounded were carried in, but Corporal O'Brien died of his wounds and was later buried behind the lines in the cemetery at the Citadel.

In what Sassoon admits was a somewhat foolhardy exercise he later retraced his steps towards the German trenches; as he searched for abandoned weapons he narrowly avoided being killed by a mortar bomb which fortunately passed over his head. His part in the night's action earned him a recommendation for a Military Cross.

In *Goodbye to All That*, Graves wrote that Sassoon was known throughout the Division as 'Mad Jack' and this description is widely used and accepted whenever mention is made of Sassoon's undoubted courage in this and other actions. However, Julian Dadd told Sassoon that he had never heard of him being referred to in that manner; Sassoon was known in the regiment as 'Kangaroo' (no doubt a reference to his considerable height). As regards any suggestion of 'madness' in the exploit that gained him the Military Cross, Dadd goes on to say that it would be difficult to imagine a word more inappropriate to describe Sassoon's calm and logical activity on the night of 25 May 1916.

From time to time the Army would put on a concert for the enjoyment of the troops, when the war could be forgotten for a short time - many writers later mentioned such entertainments in their personal memoirs, including Graves, Sassoon and Edmund Blunden. The quality of the performers was not always high but usually one or

Citadel New Military Cemetery Fricourt. The British front line of 1 July 1916 ran across the skyline, with the Bois Français trenches on the extreme left.

two in the battalion who could play a musical instrument, tell jokes (often in doubtful taste) or recite, would entertain their companions as best they could. Early in June, and just before Sassoon was due for leave, he attended a very successful concert run by the Royal Welch on spare ground at the rear of the Quartermaster's Store in Morlancourt. The 7th Division Band

Corporal O'Brien's grave at Citadel New Military Cemetery near Fricourt.

The Citadel: a view from the location of the Bois Français front line trenches in May-July 1916, looking south to the British rear areas and away from No Man's Land around the Kiel Trench sector. Although it lay within range of the German artillery, the ground was invisible to them and was therefore useful to the British as a dump for supplies to be carried to the front line by working parties. After 1 July 1916 the whole of the Citadel area was greatly enlarged, with supply dumps and troop accommodation covering the fields.

CITADEL NEW MILITARY CEMETERY

took part and one of the individual performers was the well-known actor Captain Basil Hallam Radford, then serving in the Kite-Balloon Section of the Royal Flying Corps.

CAPTAIN BASIL HALLAM RADFORD RFC
('The Knut with a K')

Basil Hallam (his stage name) was an accomplished and very popular West End music hall artist of great charm who was accepted by the aristocracy, including Raymond Asquith, the Prime Minister's son, and Lady Diana Manners (later Lady Diana Cooper). On medical grounds he need not have enlisted, but when he did so he was commissioned in the Kite-Balloon

A French Cacquot type kite-balloon about to go aloft. Designed by a French officer, Captain Cacquot, this type of balloon was aerodynamically superior to earlier designs. The British Army adopted it for use in Palestine as well as along the Western Front. Basil Hallam Radford was killed as he tried to extricate himself from a balloon of this type. The same design was used in the Second World War for balloon barrages, set up by the RAF as a deterrent to low-flying enemy aircraft and flying bombs.

Basil Hallam Radford.

Section of the Royal Flying Corps. On 20 August 1916, not far from Beaumont Hamel, Radford's observation balloon had reached some 6000 feet when it broke free from its winch cable and began to drift towards No Man's Land. His companion, Second Lieutenant P. B. Moxon, was the first to jump from the balloon's basket, Radford sitting on its rim waiting for Moxon's parachute to open. It is not clear what then took place, except that Radford apparently made his descent without his parachute. The Brigade Medical Officer, Dr W. B. Purchase (later a London Coroner), considered Radford's death was probably caused by his getting caught in the parachute's lines as he jumped clear of the basket causing him to be strangled. He was 28 years old. It so happened that Raymond Asquith, the Prime Minister's son, saw it take place and wrote to Lady Diana reporting, somewhat casually, that he was able to identify the body by means of Radford's cigarette case. He is buried in Couin British Cemetery.

Kite balloon being prepared for flight. The Royal Flying Corps observer is attached to his parachute, which hangs outside the basket.

Sassoon continued to play his part in Battalion routine, leading working parties to reconstruct the sandbagged trenches and sometimes out in front of the British wire defences, supervising their never-ending repair. He returned from ten days' leave on 19 June to a scene of much military activity on both sides. By the evening of 27 June the Battalion was back in the front line with Sassoon's C company dispersed on carrying duties. The 'Big Show' was about to begin, but not before agreeable news arrived next day that the recommendation for the award of a Military Cross to Sassoon had been approved.

Back in the Royal Welch Fusiliers' Depot in Liverpool (following the operation on his nose), Graves and his fellow officers awaited orders for France as replacements for the inevitable casualties. They would soon be needed.

Chapter Four

THE BATTLE OF THE SOMME

Saturday 1 July 1916 on the Somme battlefield has been described as the British Army's blackest day of the Great War, for by nightfall it had suffered over 57,000 casualties for virtually no ground gained. The more positive features of the day were the successful assaults by the 7th, 18th and 30th Divisions between Maricourt and Fricourt, a front of five miles in length on the right of the British line - attacks in which the 1st Royal Welch of the 7th Division in the Bois Français trenches played a vital part.

The British offensive at Fricourt, which was carried out with tremendous courage by all the battalions taking part, had its share of defeat and disaster. The 10th West Yorkshires, for example, achieved

Bois Français trenches.

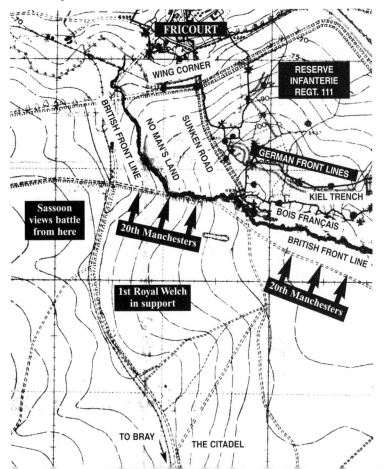

KIEL TRENCH

Bois Français trench line. Taken from the location of the British rear of May-July 1916. The line of trees on the horizon marks the German front line trenches of that time. Two small isolated trees to the left centre mark Point 110 New Military Cemetery.

the unenviable distinction of having the highest number of casualties suffered by any battalion on 1 July - an astonishing 710, with just 31 men still able to answer the roll call at the end of the day.

The attack from the Bois Français trenches was to be undertaken by the 5th Manchester Pals under the Battalion commander, Lieutenant-Colonel Lewis. The 1st Royal Welch were in various positions in support: Sassoon's C Company, for instance, took up a position near Fricourt cemetery and was detailed to act as a carrying company. With no duties allocated to him, Sassoon decided to watch the battle from Crawley Ridge, a piece of high ground overlooking the battlefield about 500 yards to the rear of the British trenches. From here he could see what was happening on his left towards Fricourt, and also watch the assault to be made by the 20th Manchesters from the Bois Français area during their attack, timed for the afternoon. The soldiers holding the German front, belonging to Reserve-Infanterie-Regiment No. 111 of the 28th Reserve Division, were to prove formidable opponents. Sassoon's friend Julian Dadd was placed in command of the Brigade's Mobile Reserve.

A and B Companies of the Manchesters, now facing the enemy trenches, held the left of the Battalion's front, with D Company to their right in the Battalion's central position with C Company further to the right. Between them they occupied the line as far as the trenches facing the enemy in Kiel Trench, the scene of Sassoon's exploit on 25 May. A

lane from the Citadel passed through D Company's position, entered No Man's Land and then descended fairly steeply to form a sunken road leading to the crossroads on the Mametz - Fricourt road. Here the Germans had established an infamous strong point, known to the British as Wing Corner, which was to take a heavy toll of the attacking British troops. Two formidable German positions to the right of the sunken road were known as Sunken Road Trench and The Rectangle.

The trenches to the left of the Manchesters were occupied by the 7th Green Howards, a Yorkshire regiment, with another from the same county, the 10th West Yorks, on the Green Howards' left flank. Both battalions were directly opposite the heavily defended village of Fricourt. The Manchesters' right flank was held by the 2nd Borders. Beyond them, and facing Mametz, were the 9th Devons and 2nd Gordon Highlanders, which together with the 2nd Borders belonged to 20th Brigade. Brigadier-General Minshull Ford, formerly the Commanding Officer of the 1st Royal Welch, was now in command of the 91st Brigade which was composed of two Manchester Pals battalions (21st and 22nd Manchesters) together with the 1st South Staffs. and 2nd Queens.

The brunt of the British attack in the Mametz sector was to be borne by Minshull Ford's battalions. Both Minshull Ford and Lieutenant-Colonel Stockwell, now commanding the 1st Royal Welch, had served as subalterns in the Regiment in pre-war days and so were on friendly terms. On this basis Stockwell asked for his superior's opinion as to the likelihood of success on 1 July: Minshull Ford was highly optimistic while Stockwell, realising that progress in the Mametz sector was vital in order to cut off the enemy holding Fricourt, was not so sure. With

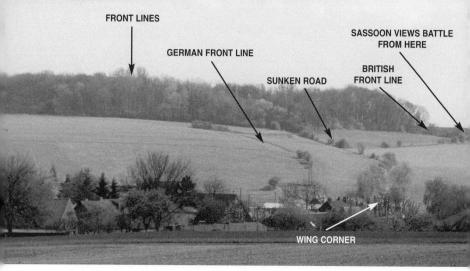

FRONT LINES

GERMAN FRONT LINE

SASSOON VIEWS BATTLE
FROM HERE

SUNKEN ROAD

BRITISH
FRONT LINE

WING CORNER

Bois Français with Fricourt village, showing the position of front lines on 1 July 1916. The field in the foreground is the site of the West Yorkshires' disastrous charge towards the German lines on the edge of the village.

this in mind the 20th Manchesters (5th Pals) and the 7th Green Howards were ordered not to attack with the main body at 7.30 am but to await further instructions for an attack in the afternoon.

By 7.0 a.m. on 1 July 1916 the British bombardment had reached its climax. Just before the guns lifted at 7.30 am, three British mines were exploded under the German front line opposite Fricourt and two companies of the 10th West Yorks immediately swept forward across No Man's Land and past the craters, reaching the German trench line almost without loss.

It was now the turn of the remainder of the 10th West Yorks. to support their comrades. Unfortunately, the bombardment had not

Direction of attacks, 1 July 1916, at Bois Français and Fricourt.

1ST ROYAL WELCH ATTACK LATER
EVENTUALLY ENTERING FRICOURT

DIRECTION OF 20TH
MANCHESTERS
AFTERNOON ATTACK

DIRECTION OF 10TH WEST YORKSHIRES MORNING ATTACK.

eliminated the German machine-gun posts at two positions on the battalion's right flank: firstly at the German Tambour trenches, where the bombardment had lifted and moved forward after the enemy had emerged from their deep dug-outs (creeping barrages would not be the norm for another three months) and secondly, the notorious German machine-gun post at Wing Corner was for some reason not fired on at all by the designated Field Artillery battery. It therefore remained in action throughout most of the day and continued to inflict very heavy casualties on the attacking British troops.

What followed was inevitable: the support companies of the 10th West Yorks met devastating fire from these two machine-gun posts and were mown down. The West Yorks' companies in the initial assault, fighting stubbornly in the German trenches, were totally isolated and slowly overwhelmed. Both the Commanding Officer, Lieutenant-Colonel Dickson, and his Second-in-Command, Major J. Knott DSO, were killed. (Dickson and Knott were buried in Fricourt New Military cemetery; but after the war permission was given for Major Knott's body to be moved to Ypres Reservoir Cemetery in Belgium. Here he was buried alongside his brother Captain Henry Knott, who had died of wounds on 7 September 1915 whilst in action with the 9th Northumberland Fusiliers.)

As the trenches vacated by the West Yorks were now unmanned and vulnerable to any German counter-attack, orders were immediately given for the 7th East Yorks. to take over the position.

Sassoon was well-placed, as an observant man of letters, to record the events of the day for future reference. The account in *Memoirs of an Infantry Officer,* based on his diary for the day, notes that 'On July the first the weather, after an early morning mist, was of the kind commonly called heavenly.' (He follows this gently ironic appreciation with a vivid description of what it had felt like to sit underground for the past week while the final bombardment shook the air and ground and battered their minds.)

From his relatively safe location on the high ground of Crawley Ridge, Sassoon watched the initial advance of the 10th West Yorks and noted the cheers of the men of the 7th Green Howards, who were obeying orders and standing fast in the trenches next to them.

But, as if the near annihilation of the 10th West Yorks was not enough, another disaster struck. In his Battalion Orders Lieutenant-Colonel R. D. Fife, the 7th Green Howards' commanding officer, had stressed two points: that the Battalion's attack would not go over with the general assault at 7.30 am but would take place at a time to be

Wing Corner, Fricourt. Taken from the site of the German front line of 1 July 1916, facing the British front line (the row of houses on the sky-line). Major Kent and his men charged the enemy trenches from here, and were mown down. The telegraph pole marks the site of the German strong-point that caused so many casualties during the British attacks on 1 July; it was finally destroyed by the 1st Royal Welch Fusiliers bombers late that evening. The lane to the left, known as the Sunken Road, led up the hill to Bois Français area.

notified later; and that the capture of the notorious machine-gun post opposite A Company at Wing Corner was essential. In order to eliminate any misunderstanding, Colonel Fife discussed his orders with all his officers, including Major R. E. D. Kent in command of A Company. It was therefore with total astonishment that Colonel Fife learned that at 7.45 a.m. Major Kent had given orders for his company to attack the enemy lines at Wing Corner, and that in doing so he and the company had been mown down. Those who were left, including Major Kent who was wounded, were lying out in No Man's Land while the vacated trenches were practically unmanned. D Company came up from the support lines to fill the gap and took over.

Minshull Ford's battalions to the right of the 20th Manchesters were making steady if difficult progress towards Mametz. It would help them if the enemy's attention could now be directed elsewhere, and orders therefore came through that Fricourt was to be attacked at 2.30 pm. This task fell to the 20th Manchesters, who were to advance from the line at Bois Français, the remaining companies of the 7th Green Howards, who were to attack from opposite Wing Corner and the 7th East Yorks., who had taken over the West Yorks' trenches facing Fricourt. As the men were getting ready, an officer crawled back from No Man's Land to the British front line dragging the wounded Major Kent behind him. Shortly afterwards the Major was carried away for medical attention. He never returned to the battalion and the mystery as to what prompted such a flagrant disobedience of orders has never been cleared up. He eventually recovered from his wounds, was promoted to Lieutenant-Colonel and was killed in action on 27 May 1918, commanding the 4th Green Howards in the Battle of the Aisne. His name is on the Soissons Memorial.

The prospect of success for the 7th East Yorks (now manning the trenches vacated by the ill-fated 10th West Yorks) in the forthcoming attack was poor, for the enemy machine-guns at the German Tambour trenches had still not been silenced. It was no better for the remaining companies of the 7th Green Howards, because no British artillery fire could be brought down on the German machine-guns at Wing Corner: messages had come in that there were many wounded Green Howards lying in front of the position. Nevertheless, the two Yorkshire battalions were ordered to attack - with predictable results. The Green Howards left their trenches at 2.30 pm and immediately came under murderous machine-gun fire, just managing to advance 50 yards. In the three minutes it took to cover that distance they lost fifteen officers and 336 Other Ranks. Shortly after this the 7th East Yorks went forward and achieved an advance of just a few yards, losing five officers and 150 men in the process.

Like the two Yorkshire battalions, the 20th Manchesters opened their attack on Fricourt at around 2.30 pm, supported by the 1st Royal Welch's bombing company led by Lieutenants Stevens and Newton (who features in Sassoon's 'Sherston' memoirs as 'Fernby'). Under a rolling barrage the Manchesters' first wave went forward towards the sunken road and entered the German front line with just a few casualties, but in doing so lost direction and swung to the right. This brought them into the German trenches in the Bois Français, and a vicious bombing fight then ensued.

The supporting companies suffered very heavy casualties as they moved forward across No Man's Land, particularly from the dreaded German machine-guns at Wing Corner whose arc of fire encompassed not only the 7th Green Howards, now steadfastly attacking in front of them, but also the 20th Manchesters to the Germans' left as they entered the German front line. Unfortunately the bombers in this assault were annihilated, which meant that the expected bombing raids down the hill and through the Sunken Road and nearby Rectangle trenches could not take place.

These positions were strongly held and difficult to clear. Colonel Lewis of the Manchesters had gone over to assess the position, for no progress was being made by his Battalion on either flank and, following this, the Manchesters' reserves and Julian Dadd's Mobile Reserve were sent in to retrieve the situation. Colonel Lewis was killed at this time.

At 5.00 pm the 1st Royal Welch were ordered forward to assist the beleaguered Manchesters and instructed to capture the whole of the hill leading down from Bois Français to Wing Corner. This included the stubbornly held Sunken Road and Rectangle trenches. It was now that the battalion's discipline and training came into play: A and B Companies and the battalion bombers moved up from the Citadel and entered the captured trenches in the cratered area of the Bois Français front line. The initiative was soon regained, and by 5.30 pm, as he looked across from Crawley Ridge, Sassoon could see some Royal Welch crawling towards Sunken Road trench where they set off a red marker flare.

Further progress was made from the Bois Français, with the Royal Welch slowly fighting and bombing their way westwards and thence along the trenches on the hill leading down to Fricourt, and large numbers of German prisoners were taken - but it was not until 10.30 pm that Lieutenant Stevens and the Royal Welch bombers finally reached and captured Wing Corner, a position which had wrought such havoc on the British that day. After capturing the machine-gun post, the Battalion modestly described this German redoubt as 'strongly held'. A search for Colonel Lewis' body was made and he was later buried in a cemetery near Mametz.

Although the 20th Manchesters suffered 326 casualties during the day, including some 130 killed or missing, the 1st Royal Welch who joined the battle at a later stage fared better, recording four men killed and 35 wounded.

VISIT NO. 2: THE SOMME AREA - BOIS FRANÇAIS TRENCHES AND THE CITADEL

Leaving Albert on the **D938** road, continue until it crosses the **D147** on the outskirts of Fricourt. Almost immediately beyond the crossroads, turn right up a narrow lane leading up on to the escarpment that overlooks Fricourt. The posts at the turning mark, approximately, the location of the infamous 'Wing Corner' of the 1 July 1916 battle.

Stop and park at the top of the hill: you are now in the Bois Français sector of the Somme front of 1916. Although the track continues beyond this point, it is not advisable to take the car further. Follow the path straight ahead (with another track leading off along the ridge to the left), and go gently down hill. Point 110 Old cemetery lies on the right of the track, with Point 110 New shortly after it on the left. Here, on the left of the group of headstones, you will find the graves of Thomas, Pritchard and Richardson.

Turn left out of the cemetery and continue down the track for Citadel New Military cemetery (close to the Bray - Fricourt road and accessible by car from it). This is where Sassoon's NCO, Corporal O'Brien, is buried. Retrace your steps; turn right along the ridge close to the car; this takes you past the grassy remains of a Second World War anti-aircraft gun site on the left (established to protect the aeronautical engineering factory at Méaulte, near Albert). The path follows roughly the British front line of 1916; after about 200 yards, Kiel Trench can be located on the left, particularly in the winter and early spring months; refer to the map and photograph page 77.

Retrace your steps past the track down to Fricourt, to visit the grave of a French soldier, Tomasin, in the wood on the right.

Return to the car, drive back down to the D 938; turn left along it, then right at the crossroads. As this road takes you into Fricourt it passes the cemetery on the left of the road where many of the Green Howards killed in Major Kent's abortive attack on 1 July 1916 are buried. The area in front of the cemetery was the sector across which the Green Howards attacked that morning with such heavy loss.

Return to the **D 938** and turn left along it; shortly along it, turn left on the **D 64** road to Mametz.

Like the opening day of the battle, the morning of Sunday 2 July 1916 was fine and sunny, and Sassoon enjoyed lying out in the long grass where on the previous day it would have been certain death to do so. He reported in his diary that after bombardment the 1st Royal Welch were to take Fricourt later that day, but during the afternoon the Adjutant came up, very excitedly, to say that the attack had been cancelled, Fricourt had been occupied and no bombardment was to take place.

Somehow Sassoon did not realise that the previous night, and against orders, Colonel Stockwell had sent his bombing platoons into Fricourt where they had met little resistance and occupied the village. For his pains Stockwell was mildly admonished by Brigade 'for exceeding his orders'. However, unlike Major Kent of the Green Howards who disobeyed orders, Stockwell's independent initiative was highly effective and saved lives.

Both sides made good use of the welcome respite and spent the time bringing up ammunition and supplies of all kinds. Urgently needed reinforcements were despatched from British Infantry depots in France and at home, including Graves at the Royal Welch barracks in Litherland. Graves was disappointed to find that he was part of a draft destined for the 2nd Royal Welch in the line at Givenchy – he would have preferred to rejoin Sassoon and the 1st Battalion, but the 2nd Battalion had recently lost most of its B Company near Givenchy when a German mine exploded under their trenches. (Some bodies from this incident were discovered 85 years later, with one of the victims – Private Richard Clarke – being successfully identified.)

Lieutenant W. Kelsey Fry, MC, RAMC. One of Sassoon's friends, twice wounded, who served as Medical Officer to the 1st Royal Welch Fusiliers. He had a distinguished medical career after the Great War.

Sassoon went down the hill into Fricourt, by now full of British soldiers looking for souvenirs, but orders soon came through to move on to take the next objective – Mametz Wood – which was believed to be unoccupied. By the next day the 1st Royal Welch were close to the wood, and dozing appreciatively in the sunshine. Just under a mile long from north to south and some 3/4 mile wide, it was a mass of old oak and birch trees and thick undergrowth. Much of the dominating higher ground on its eastern side was vulnerable to German machine-gun fire and the eventual capture of the wood was to prove a mammoth task.

Confirmation of the award of a Military Cross to Sassoon had just come through. In a friendly gesture the Medical Officer, Lieutenant Kelsey Fry, removed the ribbon of his own M.C. from his tunic later in the afternoon and skilfully sewed it on to the uniform jacket of a highly delighted Sassoon.

Any suggestion that Mametz Wood was unoccupied was quickly dispelled, for when the 2nd Royal Irish attempted to enter the wood they ran into strong resistance and needed artillery assistance in order to extricate themselves. New orders were issued, requiring Quadrangle Wood (south of Mametz Wood) to be taken in a night assault together with Quadrangle Trench, just beyond it. Just after midnight on Tuesday 4 July, therefore, the 1st Royal Welch was sent into the line at Bottom

BOTTOM WOOD

QUADRANGLE WOOD

X

Part of the Mametz Wood battlefield. Taken from the high ground north of Mametz village, reached by the British on 1 July 1916. Quadrangle Trench, Sassoon's solo route to Mametz Wood, lay behind Quadrangle Wood and led off to the right of the picture. The cross marks the approximate place where Major-General Ingouville-Williams ('Inky Bill') was killed by shell fire on 22 July 1916. Humorists suggested that his death occurred whilst he was indulging in his troops' popular pastime of hunting souvenirs.

Wood on the Contalmaison road to the south of Mametz Wood, with the 9th Northumberland Fusiliers on their left and the Royal Irish on the right. With A and D Companies instructed to undertake the coming attack, Sassoon's C Company was again employed as a carrying company. (Sassoon's short poem 'At Carnoy', seems relevant here: dated 3 July, it describes a Brigade camp at sunset, with men playing mouth-organs and his own contentment - but he ends with '.... To-morrow we must go/To take some cursèd Wood ... O world God made!')

The assault began about 30 minutes later and was eventually successful, with a substantial contribution once more from Julian Dadd and his bombers. A light railway running through a narrow cutting into Mametz Wood created a break of about 200 yards in the captured German trench line and was easily covered by enemy machine-gun and sniper fire. The gap marked the end of Quadrangle Trench, with another one known as Wood Trench continuing the German defences and leading into the wood.

As the fighting dwindled and dawn broke Sassoon decided to leave Bottom Wood and make his way up the Contalmaison road to the captured Quadrangle Trench. Beside the light railway gap in the trench line separating Quadrangle and Wood trenches a Royal Welch bombing

87

2nd Lieutenant V.F. Newton 1st Royal Welch Fusiliers (Sassoon's 'Fernby'). After her son's death Colonel Stockwell wrote to his mother about the 1st RWF's actions in the Delville Wood/Ginchy area in which Lieutenant Newton was involved: 'A charming boy - always very keen and full of pluck; so much so that I especially selected him to go to the grenadier company, the picked company of the battalion. He did some splendid work with the bombs on the 26th-27th August 1916 when he had some very severe fighting and on the day he was wounded he was in command of the battalion bombers...'

2nd Lieutenant V.F. Newton. A cardboard replica of the original wooden cross placed on Lieutenant Newton's grave in 1916. It was thought to have been made by his mother.

post was commanded by Second Lieutenant Newton ('Fernby' in Sassoon's *Memoirs of an Infantry Officer*).

Sassoon had not been there long before snipers opened fire, and men were killed and wounded as they tried to deepen the captured trenches. Instructing Newton to order his men to continue digging, a furious Sassoon picked up a bag of Mills bombs, crossed the light railway track, and climbed up the opposite slope of the railway cutting. He then proceeded to bomb his way along Wood Trench towards the edge of Mametz Wood, scattering the fifty or sixty surprised German soldiers who were digging there. His dramatic solo advance was supported by Newton's Lewis gun team, which opened fire on the retreating Germans as opportunity arose.

Sassoon's one-man attack on Mametz Wood, seen from the July 1916 site of Quadrangle Trench. The small bush on the former railway embankment in the middle distance marks the approximate point where Sassoon met 'Fernby' before entering Wood Trench, where he surprised German soldiers. The edge of Quadrangle Wood appears on the right.

LANCE CORPORAL J. GIBSON – 'KENDLE'

In Sassoon's fictional account of his bombing dash down Wood Trench (in *Memoirs of an Infantry Officer*), we are told that 'Kendle'was killed by a sniper shot just above his eyes. One of Sassoon's biographers mentions Gibson's death on 5 July 1916: the suggestion seems to be that Sassoon was so upset by this death that he felt he must avenge it by chasing the enemy down Wood Trench - but his Diary makes no mention of being accompanied in this exploit. A footnote in Sassoon's diary for June 30 1916 gives Gibson's date of death as 16 July 1916; official records state that No 24460 L/Cpl James Gibson, from Whitehaven, in Cumbria, died of wounds on 23 July 16. It would seem that the Lance Corporal was wounded in the Battalion's action at Bazentin on 16 July and later died of his wounds. (He is buried in Heilly Station cemetery.)

In the fictional *Memoirs* Sassoon describes how, instead of gaining congratulations for bombing the trench, he was disconcerted to be firmly reprimanded for the exploit - both for undertaking it without telling his superior officer, and for failing to consolidate his gain. In *Goodbye to All That* Graves describes the incident and adds that after clearing the enemy trench, instead of signalling or reporting the incident Sassoon sat down quietly to read poetry and, by representing 'British patrols still out', delayed the attack on Mametz Wood.

It was now 6.0 a.m. and time to return. Slowly he made his way back to Quadrangle Trench, passing Newton and his men on the way and later going on to Battalion HQ at Bottom Wood.

Mametz Wood battlefield, taken from the approximate position reached by the British on 1 July 1916, looking down at Mametz Wood. It was not until 12 July that the wood was cleared of the enemy and the advance resumed towards Bazentin.

Clearly, the Germans were not going to give up Quadrangle Trench without a fight and around this time they launched a counter attack from their support line, using a long communication trench called Quadrangle Alley which led to the 1st Royal Welch holding Quadrangle Trench. As the communication trench was rather shallow the heads of the approaching enemy could be easily seen as they came to the blocked end of the trench. The Royal Welch immediately opened up with Lewis guns and the bombing platoon drove the attackers back the way they had come, gaining some 300 yards of trench and seizing a new vantage point over the German front line which enabled them to repulse further German assaults promptly. It was around this time that Sassoon drafted his poem 'Counter-attack'. It was completed in Scotland in the summer of 1917, and is one of his most uncompromisingly bitter evocations of the waste and horror of front-line life.

By nightfall on 5 July the Battalion, now down to 400 men, had handed over at Bottom Wood to its sister battalion the 14th Royal Welch, with double the complement of men, under the command of Lieutenant-Colonel Gwyther. Stockwell and Gwyther knew each other, having served together before the war. This Battalion was recruited in Llandudno and its surrounding area, part of the 38th (Welsh) Division soon to receive its baptism of fire.

It is interesting to read the comment of a 14th Royal Welch officer

90

TO THE BAZENTINS

who actually took part in that relief at Bottom Wood and to have his opinion of the senior Battalion. He reported that in all his war-time service he had never seen a battalion depart more promptly on being relieved, remarking that as soon as the 14th Royal Welch appeared the men of the 1st Battalion were up and away as fast as they could manage. (The same officer does, however, go on to observe that in the light of his later military experience he could well see why they did so!) In the meantime, the 1st Royal Welch marched back to Heilly for a much-needed rest, arriving there on 6 July to shelter for a few days in very swampy conditions in brown painted tents. The break would not last long.

Next day the preliminaries began for the capture of Mametz Wood by the 38th (Welsh) Division. This involved four battalions of the 52nd Division, two of which (the 10th Lancashire Fusiliers and the 9th

Communications trench near Mametz Wood. The 38th (Welsh) Division were assisted in their attacks on Mametz Wood by the capture of the village of Contalmaison nearby. The picture shows captured German officers and men under escort, some of them filing down a trench near Mametz Wood not far from the village.

Mametz Wood and the Dragon Memorial: taken from the high ground overlooking Happy Valley and Mametz Wood in 1996, on the 80th anniversary of the attack by the 38th (Welsh) Division. The Dragon Memorial commemorates the men who fell in actions here in July 1916. Both Sassoon and Graves moved up to the front line with the 1st and 2nd Royal Welch through this valley after the capture of the wood.

Northumberland Fusiliers) undertook a night attack from the recently captured Quadrangle Trench against the German support lines. The enemy were well prepared, and after heavy fighting the battalions were forced to withdraw. Next, the 12th Manchesters and 9th Duke of Wellingtons were ordered to stage another assault on these German support lines, this time in broad daylight - which, not surprisingly, immediately attracted heavy machine-gun fire from Mametz Wood. Both battalions suffering heavy casualties. The 7th East Yorks, now reinforced after their recent casualties at Fricourt, almost succeeded in capturing part of the support lines but - like the other battalions - was driven back by enemy fire from Mametz Wood.

Another attack was mounted on the opposite side of the wood, by the 16th Welch and 11th South Wales Borderers of the 38th (Welsh) Division, starting from the vulnerable up-hill position known as Caterpillar Wood. Heavy enemy fire from Mametz Wood drove both battalions back with heavy casualties; the 10th Borderers resumed the attack in the afternoon but that also failed after Lieutenant-Colonel Smith, their Commanding Officer, was killed. Orders came through that the 17th Royal Welch must now take over the offensive, but caution prevailed: their attack was cancelled and they were merely required to hold the trenches at Caterpillar Wood.

One of the battalions in the previous night's attack was the London Welch (15th Royal Welch Fusiliers) in which the artist/poet No. 22579 Private W. David Jones was serving. Late that night the battalion had reached the edge of the wood at its junction with Wood Trench, the scene of Sassoon's recent exploit, when it was forced back. Jones was wounded in the left leg during this action, and later invalided home.

DAVID JONES 1895-1974

Poet and artist, yet another highly creative member of the Royal Welch Fusiliers. At the outbreak of war Jones, then a student at Camberwell School of Art, made several attempts to join the army, being refused first by the Artists Rifles and then by the Montgomery and Welsh Horse Yeomanry (later to become the 25th Royal Welch Fusiliers in which Sassoon served in 1918). A letter from his father to Lloyd George resulted in Jones being enlisted in the 15th Royal Welch Fusiliers (London Welch) on 2 January 1915. By the end of the year the Battalion was in France and subsequently served in the Laventie sector, where in May 1916 they gave trench instruction to the poet Ivor Gurney's battalion of the Gloucestershire Regiment. Gurney described the London Welch as '....the nicest people you could meet - and educated'. After being wounded at Mametz Wood in July 1916 Jones returned in October 1916 to active service with a Field Survey Company in the Ypres Salient. A few months later he rejoined the London Welch and fought with them in the Battle of Pilckem on 31 July 1917. From September 1917 to early 1918 he served with his battalion in the Bois Grenier area, but fell ill with trench fever and returned to England. Next he was sent to the Royal Welch's barracks in Limerick until his discharge in January 1919; he remained a private soldier throughout his four years of army service

His literary interpretation of his war experiences took longer than most, for he did not embark on his great prose poem *In Parenthesis* until 1927 and it was not published for another ten years. This remarkable distillation of war, Catholicism, Welsh and Arthurian legend, human nature and much more, is dense with reference and reflection, but it includes a poetic and vivid description of what it felt like to be in Mametz Wood in the thick of the fighting in July 1916.

The Army had never anticipated that the capture of a wood could be so difficult. A total of eight battalions had now been involved and still Mametz Wood remained in German hands: some senior officers were replaced and a fresh attempt to go forward was launched on 11 July, with some units now under new commanders.

In terrible and exhausting conditions fierce hand-to-hand fighting carried on until finally, just after mid-day on 12 July, Mametz Wood was clear of the enemy. In those three days it had taken at least eleven battalions from three regiments - Welch, Royal Welch, and South Wales Borderers - to achieve this result. The cost to the 38th (Welsh) Division in taking the wood was high, for they had suffered 4,000 casualties, of which some 600 were killed or missing. The Royal Welch alone lost two battalion commanders killed in action and two more, including Stockwell's friend Lieutenant-Colonel Gwyther, severely wounded - regular army officers whose invaluable experience was now lost.

The Godbert, Amiens. Now a theatre, this was a popular restaurant in the Great War, much frequented by officers on leave from the front, including Sassoon and others from his battalion.

There was one particularly devastating personal loss, when one man's actions indirectly caused the death of his own brother. Following an order from Captain Wyn Griffith, on the 38th (Welsh) Division staff working with Brigade, a runner was detailed to take his message to stop an artillery bombardment; on this occasion the runner was Griffith's young brother Private W.E.O. Griffith of the 17th Royal Welch - who was killed as he returned from delivering the message. His name is on the Thiepval Memorial.

In these challenging circumstances the Division had done remarkably well, but in the eyes of the Army not well enough, for valuable time had been lost which allowed the Germans to prepare for the next advance - a delay which was to prove costly in the forthcoming British attacks.

One of the central reasons that shaped the preparation for the Battle of the Somme had been the urgent need to relieve the French army, hard-pressed by the constant German attacks at Verdun. It was at the peak of the battle for Mametz Wood that an event of great significance took place far away to the south at Verdun: because of the serious situation on the Somme, when the German General Falkenhayn arrived just north of the city he immediately ordered numerous artillery units to be sent north to reinforce the German forces engaged in the Somme battle - thus vindicating one of the main objectives of the British offensive.

On 7 July, while the attack on Mametz Wood was under preparation, Sassoon and some fellow officers, including the battalion Quartermaster 'Joe' Cotterill and Julian Dadd, rode to Fourth Army Headquarters in the grounds of the elegant château at Querrieu. The Fourth Army's Quartermaster here was Captain E.A. Parker, whose place in the 1st Royal Welch Cotterill had temporarily taken. Both Parker and Cotterill had been with the Battalion in pre-war days, and in view of the connection, Parker willingly provided motor transport for Sassoon and his friends to drive on to Amiens, have an excellent lunch at the Godbert restaurant and a pleasant day's sightseeing in the city.

By 13 July the Battalion was on the move again, this time to join in the battle for the next series of woods at Bazentin. The next day Sassoon met Graves at Bécordel near Fricourt and had a long talk with him, the 2nd Royal Welch having recently arrived there ready to take part in the Somme battles. They parted next day.

VISIT NO. 3: MAMETZ

Enter Mametz village on the **D 64** road and turn left at the cross roads, beside the war memorial. (C4 - sign to Contalmaison and 38 Welsh Division Memorial). Some 500 m down the road, fork right at the 38th Welsh Division Memorial sign and follow a farm track (good surface) for more than half a mile to the Dragon memorial. (Car parking and turning space.) The large wood facing the dramatic red dragon on its plinth is Mametz Wood, the scene of much heavy fighting early in July 1916; this is the area in which Graves and Sassoon were serving in the middle of that month, and was known as Happy Valley.

Return to the car, retrace your route back to the road and turn right towards Contalmaison. The small wood on the left, 200m down the road, was known to Sassoon and his men as Bottom Wood. Continue on: the next wood on the right, another 300 m along the road, was Quadrangle Wood; pause here and look to the right across the fields towards the edge of Mametz Wood beyond. This was the scene of Sassoon's venture towards the wood, throwing bombs at the retreating Germans.

Continue forward and enter Contalmaison village,

In front of the large church, rebuilt in the 1920s, turn right on the **D 20** for about 1.5 km. This takes you past the substantial bulk of Mametz Wood again, on your right, where Graves was taken after being wounded on 20 July 1916.

Beyond the wood and at the bottom of a gentle slope, turn left on the D 73 into Bazentin-le-Petit. The first and very sharp right turn (with CWGC sign) takes you into a small lane; park the car at the end and walk up the path to the British and communal cemetery at the end. This is approximately where Graves was badly wounded on 20 July 1916. Return to the car, go back up the lane, and turn right.

A Different Kind of Memorial

As you turn right out of the lane, look across the road to observe a very unusual memorial: tall, thin and open, it is a modern commemoration of the great 18th century naturalist Lamarck, who was born in Bazentin. Because of his early studies of giraffes, the memorial represents a giraffe - but the materials used are car and motor-bike parts! It is a striking and witty compliment to an original thinker whose conclusions are still studied and referred to in discussion of Darwinian theories.

Drive up through the village and at the top turn right along the narrow road that leads towards High Wood (Bois des Fourcaux). Note the private memorial on the right to Captain Wallace, of the 10th Worcesters, who was killed in action on 22 July 1916. It was along this road that Graves found the men of the Gordons who had died in the recent battle for High Wood.

Turn right at the end, passing London cemetery on your right and High Wood on the left, the scene of very heavy fighting through the summer of 1916. The area to the right was where the Deccan Horse made their memorable charge on 14 July 1916.

At the junction **turn left** on to the **D 20**, noting the memorial to 'Bristol's Own' at the corner. Coming in to Longueval, turn right on the D 20 and at the fork turn left, passing Delville Wood on the left, the CWGC cemetery on the right and then the South African memorial and museum on the left. (The wood can be explored on foot; one tree, behind the museum, is a survivor of the 1916 fighting.) On the road, the end of the wood is approximately where Edmund Dadd was killed. It was also in the trenches here that Julian Dadd, Kelsey Fry and Newton were wounded.

Reverse direction; on the right, just past the cemetery, turn into the café/visitor centre car park (refreshments, memorabilia, toilets).

Chapter Five

THE SOMME CONTINUES

The British Army's heavy losses on 1 July 1916 led to an immediate call for reinforcements to be sent out to France. Much to his disappointment, Graves was drafted not to the 1st Battalion but to the 2nd Royal Welch further north, holding the line at the Duck's Bill trenches at Givenchy where he arrived on 5 July in the midst of a reprisal raid on the German lines. Urgent needs for reinforcements frequently overrode the official attachment of officers and men to their regiment and in this case, as victims of an administrative convenience, the Royal Welch found that they had a substantial draft of men from the King's Shropshire Light Infantry. After later negotiations all the Shropshire men rejoined a battalion of their regiment, while half the number of Welshmen were sent over to the Royal Welch.

On 20 June, when the 2nd Royal Welch took over from the 4th Suffolks, they were assured that the line at the Duck's Bill was now free of German mining activity; but around 2.00 am two days later they suffered very heavy casualties when the Germans exploded a mine

Lieutenant-Colonel W. H. Stanway (late 2nd Royal Welch Fusiliers) with his officers of the 6th Cheshires. Almost immediately after the action at the Red Dragon Crater in June 1916, Stanway was promoted to Lieutenant-Colonel and made Commanding Officer of the 6th Cheshires. Believed to have been taken in 1917, this group shows him wearing the cap badge of the South Wales Borderers, the regiment into which he was eventually gazetted. Stanway is sitting in the middle of the second row.

under 'B' Company. This was immediately followed by a bombardment principally designed to prevent support troops being brought up, and then by a German raiding party some 150 strong. After some furious hand-to-hand fighting the position was eventually stabilised, Acting Major Stanway playing a great part in driving back the raiders.

ACTING MAJOR W. H. STANWAY

A veteran of the Boer War, Stanway had been a Company Sergeant Major with the 2nd Royal Welch in 1914 but by June 1916 had reached the rank of Captain (Acting Major). Early in July 1916 he was promoted to the rank of Lieutenant-Colonel, taking command of the 6th Cheshires, later being wounded during the Battalion's action at St. Julien in 1917. At the end of the war he reverted to the rank of Captain in the South Wales Borderers having won the DSO and Bar and M.C: clearly a brave and distinguished officer.

The resulting crater, measuring 120 yards long by 70 feet wide and 30 feet deep, was the largest crater on the Western Front at the time. Its

Red Dragon Mine Crater, Givenchy. A recent photograph taken from the site of the German front line in 1916. The British trenches lay along the line of trees in the background. The crater erupted on the left of the road, enveloping B Company 2nd Royal Welch Fusiliers and causing heavy casualties. One body, 2nd Lieutenant Crosland, was discovered during ploughing in 1926. Determined to take revenge, the battalion mounted a very successful raid on German trenches at The Warren, nearby, a few days later, on the day that Robert Graves joined the battalion. The body of Sergeant Hackett, VC, of 254 Tunnelling Company RE, trapped below ground when the mine exploded, lies somewhere in the field to the right of the road.

Red Dragon Crater Site. The 5th Scottish Rifles were holding the front line to the extreme left of the view shown here, next to the 2nd Royal Welch Fusiliers. On 22 June 1916, when the German mine exploded and whilst the Royal Welch were consolidating the crater lip, Sergeant Erskine of the Scottish Rifles rushed out into No Man's Land. He rescued some of the wounded here and was awarded the Victoria Cross for his bravery.

name, 'Red Dragon', from the design of the regiment's cap badge, became the Army name for the crater.

Several men of No. 254 Tunnelling Company R.E. were buried alive by the explosion as they worked in a mine shaft, including Sergeant William Hackett who was later awarded a posthumous Victoria Cross for refusing to leave a wounded comrade trapped underground. The same award was won by Sergeant J. Erskine of the 5th Scottish Rifles for bringing in men from No Man's Land, wounded when the enemy mine was detonated.

The 2nd Royal Welch were enraged by the loss of so many of their comrades in B Company, for there were over 100 casualties, one of whom, a popular 19 year old Second Lieutenant from Sandhurst, Trevor Crosland, was buried by debris. It was quickly decided that on their return to the Givenchy trenches they must undertake some form of retaliation. A large raiding party was assembled with Captains Moody and Higginson contributing their considerable local knowledge and expertise. The place selected was the German trench line to the left of Red Dragon Crater

Sergeant John Erskine, VC.

99

2nd Lieutenant T.A. Crosland, 2nd Royal Welch Fusiliers. Killed in action at the Red Dragon Crater, 22nd June 1916.

known as The Warren, consisting, among other defences, of three mine craters and numerous dug-outs. The night of the raid was deliberately fixed for 5 July 1916, according to the battalion history, 'after the opening of the Somme Offensive'. The raiding party, which was mainly equipped with bombs and hand weapons such as bill-hooks and pikes, indulged in whole-hearted destruction, blowing up German dug-outs and mine shafts. The whole attack was deemed a great success and drew the congratulations of Sir Douglas Haig.

There was sadness in the ranks, however, for a pair of brothers of whom one had been killed in the raid. His Sergeant-Major, CSM Fox, relates that 'the survivor nearly went out of his mind when he found out'. (After a similar episode at Rouen in February 1917, Sassoon wrote the savagely ironic 'Lamentations', about a soldier who 'howled and beat his chest./And, all because his brother had gone west'.) Among the awards following this action, Captain Moody received a bar to his Military Cross, and Captain Higginson a Military Cross.

PROMOTION FROM THE RANKS

Early in January 1915 Corporal Percy Moody and Private John Victor Higginson, both of the Artists' Rifles, reported to the Royal Welch still wearing their Other Rank uniforms. They were given leave to buy officers' kit and were drafted to the 2nd Royal Welch where they were to give distinguished service, both achieving the rank of Captain. Captain Higginson, who succumbed to war wounds and died in September 1919, is buried in St. Mary's Churchyard, Knockin, Shropshire.

In January 1917 Sassoon had a visit from Moody at the Depot in Litherland and described him as '....being on leave from the 2nd Battalion with two years' trench service and an M.C. and Bar. A little nonentity with a pudding face and black hair, but a stout soldier and worthy of his laurels'.

The Commanding Officer of the 2nd Royal Welch was now Lieutenant-Colonel Crawshay who had been the adjutant at the Depot in 1915 and whose eventual approval had qualified Graves for transfer to France. Graves arrived too late to take part in the raid, but was nevertheless asked by Crawshay to write out a detailed description of the event just for the Regimental records. Four days later the Battalion entrained for Amiens and upon arrival began its march to the front, with squadrons of British and Indian cavalry passing them. These were the 7th Dragoon Guards and the 20th Deccan Horse (Indian Army) on their way to assemble for an attack on High Wood. At Bécordel, where the Battalion arrived on 14 July, they learned that the 33rd Division was in reserve and that they were to be the reserve battalion of the reserve Brigade, a pleasant state of affairs not likely to continue. The others in the brigade were the 1st Scottish Rifles, 5th/6th Scottish Rifles and 20th Royal Fusiliers (referred to by Graves as 'the Chocolate Soldiers').

20th ROYAL FUSILIERS

This battalion's full title was the 20th (University & Public Schools) Battalion Royal Fusiliers. Formed in September 1914 by the High Master of Manchester Grammar School and the Lord Mayor of Manchester, it was composed almost entirely of men from Manchester University, Manchester Grammar School and various public schools - indeed it was a qualification that to join the battalion a recruit had to have attended a school listed in the Public Schools Year Book for 1913. In November 1915 they left Tidworth Barracks in Hampshire for the La Bassée front. Many of the men in its ranks were eminently suitable for commissions, but a combination of a desire 'to stick together' and the Commanding Officer's reluctance to approve applications for transfer ensured that the battalion kept its original recruits. The 2nd Royal Welch's nickname for them, the Chocolate Soldiers, was based on the contents of the very many parcels which they regularly received from well-to-do relatives.

Eventually, the Battalion was almost wiped out in its attack on High Wood on 20th July 1916, some 700 reinforcements being required on 24 July to replace those killed and wounded, very many of the dead having no known grave. In *Goodbye to All That* Graves commented insultingly - and inaccurately - on the two Scottish battalions fighting alongside the 20th Royal Fusiliers in High Wood on that day. In the case of the Scottish Rifles he wrote to Edmund Blunden in the 1930s (who had raised the matter), making a suitable retraction, but by that time there was nobody left from the 20th Royal Fusiliers to insist on a similar retraction over their behaviour.

With the capture of Mametz Wood on 12 July, orders came to move

A platoon section of the 20th (University and Public Schools) Bn Royal Fusiliers, 1915, Tidworth Barracks. The soldier at the far right was to win the MM at La Bassée in 1916, the first in the battalion to do so. He died soon after during the struggle to capture High Wood, in which the battalion lost over 700 men. Robert Graves referred to the battalion, which consisted almost entirely of ex-public school pupils, as 'The Chocolate Soldiers'.

The same view today

forward to the next stage, a surprise dawn attack on Bazentin-le Grand and Bazentin-le-Petit, including the cemetery of the latter. One of the battalions involved was the 1st Royal Welch, although Sassoon was not with them on this occasion. At dawn on 14 July the battalion made its way through the valley east of Mametz Wood known to the troops as 'Happy Valley' (and to some as 'Death Valley'), and was soon heavily engaged. By the evening, together with the 2nd Gordon Highlanders and the 2nd Royal Irish they had successfully established a new front line on the ridge facing High Wood and Longueval, joining up with units of the 3rd Division on their right. At the end of the assault the 1st Royal Welch had lost two officers killed, three wounded and 50 Other Ranks killed and wounded, whilst the Royal Irish suffered more than 300 casualties.

Before the attack the British had been told by a French General that what was proposed was quite impossible to achieve, a comment that elicited an airy response from Rawlinson's chief of staff that if his men were not on the Longueval ridge by the following morning, he would

The Bazentin area, showing the 1st and 2nd Royal Welch Fusiliers' operations in July 1916.

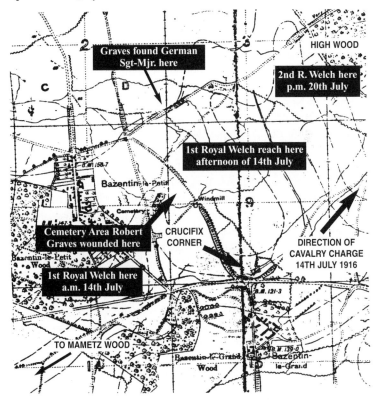

HIGH WOOD

High Wood and Delville Wood, taken from the approximate location of the British front line on 20 July 1916. It was on the road on the left that Robert Graves discovered the body of the German Sergeant Major, facing the refuges dug out of the embankment at the roadside by wounded Gordon Highlanders.

'eat his hat'. With success achieved, for valuable ground had been won, the French general generously indicated that there was no need for Major General Montgomery to eat his hat.

It had been a costly but satisfactory day; advances had been made, the South Africans had a toe-hold in Delville Wood and part of Longueval village had been captured. But High Wood lay ahead, threatening. Now, it was thought, was the ideal opportunity to send in the cavalry to help the infantry moving towards High Wood – and so at 7.0 pm the 20th Deccan Horse and the 7th Dragoon Guards, noted so recently by Graves as they moved up to the front, were sent into action. Passing through Happy Valley and thence to Crucifix Corner at Bazentin, with lances drawn they moved off the road and charged forward at full gallop across shell-pocked fields towards the right hand side of High Wood. Amazingly, they made good progress despite machine-gun fire from nearby Delville Wood, as German soldiers surrendered at the sight and others were killed in the charge. Inevitably, machine-gun emplacements beyond the wood came into action and the surviving men and horses were forced to withdraw to the cover of a nearby road. Early next morning, protected by early mist, the cavalrymen were ordered to the rear: their attack had cost them casualties of 102 officers and men, and the loss of 130 horses.

While his Battalion was engaged at Bazentin, Sassoon was able to

DELVILLE WOOD

meet Graves, recently arrived at Bécordel with the 2nd Royal Welch. As they talked against the sound of heavy guns firing on Bazentin, Graves was particularly delighted to learn that some of the officers of the 1st Royal Welch with whom he had served in the past, such as Edmund and Julian Dadd, were still alive. Later Graves briefly met Edmund Dadd, now a Captain and commanding A Company, who told him that he did not expect to survive for much longer - an accurate forecast, for he was indeed killed near Delville Wood, in the battle for Ginchy early in September.

CAPTAIN EDMUND DADD, MC

Edmund Dadd was one of three sons of Stephen Thomas Dadd, an artist, and his wife Eva. His brothers were Stephen, killed in Gallipoli, and Julian who also served in the same battalion of the Royal Welch. Before the war Edmund had served for five years in the Queen's Westminster Rifles, a Territorial Force unit, rejoining them on 3 August 1914 and going out to France with them the following November. Promoted to sergeant, he was soon recommended for a commission and in due course was gazetted Second Lieutenant in the Royal Welch Fusiliers after just one month's course of instruction. By July 1916 he had reached the rank of Captain and was awarded the Military Cross for his gallantry at Bazentin-le-Petit. In conversation with Graves at Mametz Wood when the two battalions met there, Edmund had expressed doubts about the future, mainly because he had brought his company to such a high standard of efficiency that Colonel Stockwell always seemed to use it for difficult tasks. From the many comments after his death it is clear that Dadd was a popular and efficient soldier. Stockwell wrote, 'He was my best Company Commander and was a born soldier'. Edmund's suspicions of being used for arduous duties were evidently not misplaced.

The family name is notable in a different artistic context, for their great-uncle, the well-known artist Richard Dadd, killed his own father and spent the rest of his life in a mental institution, painting the neurotically detailed but fascinating scenes of nature, fairies and elves for which he is known today.

By next morning Sassoon was back in the 1st Royal Welch transport

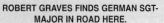

ROBERT GRAVES FINDS GERMAN SGT-MAJOR IN ROAD HERE.

lines, learning of the death and wounding of so many of his friends in the recent attacks. Very few officers now remained who had been with Sassoon six months ago: he counted a total of just seven, including the Dadd brothers. By 16 July the 1st Royal Welch had been relieved and were back in Happy Valley, an opportunity to mingle with the 2nd Royal Welch as they awaited orders to move up to High Wood.

On their way up to the front the 2nd Royal Welch had halted near Mametz Wood, the scene of so much death and destruction only a few days earlier. Rifles, equipment, wrecked railway trucks and the dead of both sides lay everywhere; friends in the 38th (Welsh) Division, many of them Royal Welch Fusiliers, were recognised and hurriedly given a decent burial in case the Battalion had to move on. Sassoon's poem 'The Road', written a month later, is a sad and clear-eyed record of the scene. Several accounts were published later of the terrible sights seen there: German snipers hanging from shell-shattered trees where they had been killed during the bombardment, and dead bodies lying where they had fallen during the fierce fighting. Both Graves and another officer later recalled going into the wood and seeing a British and German soldier still locked together in death by their bayonets, standing where they had fallen against a tree. (The scenes and atmosphere in the wood are vividly evoked by Graves in his poem 'A Dead Boche').

A captured German gun had been marked in chalk as having been taken by the 17th Royal Welch during their attack on Mametz Wood; as the 1st Royal Welch subsequently moved up to Bazentin they established it as their trophy in letters of white paint - and later still a Royal Irish inscription in even larger letters claimed the capture of the gun. Clearly the gun was felt to be an impressive prize.

DIRECTION OF CHARGE BY
DECCAN HORSE & DRAGOON
GDS 14TH JULY 1916

High Wood, a modern view taken from Caterpillar Valley Cemetery, Longueval, with High Wood in the centre horizon.

By 18 July the 2nd Royal Welch were holding the support trenches at Bazentin, between the village cemetery and the road to Martinpuich and facing High Wood about 1500 yards away. They were appalled by what they found, for the whole of the rising ground in front of them was strewn with unburied British dead. These included men of the 1st South Staffords and 2nd Queens attacks, part of the attack on High Wood that included the 7th Dragoon Guards and 20th Deccan Horse attacks of 14 July. The next day, 15 July, brought heavy casualties to the 9th Highland Light Infantry, 21st Manchesters, 1st Queens, 2nd Worcesters and a battalion of the 60th Rifles.

The Battalion had established a strong point in a lane leading directly from Bazentin to the corner of High Wood. During the capture of the village four days earlier, the 2nd Gordon Highlanders suffered casualties and some of the wounded later died where they had taken shelter, in holes hastily dug into its bank. Making his way along this lane, Graves came across a dead German Sergeant-Major - a powerfully built man with a black beard - wearing full equipment and lying on his back in the middle of the road. No talisman was available to the superstitious Graves as he walked past; the simplest protection, he felt, was to cross himself.

On 19 July orders were given for a night attack on High Wood, later postponed to a dawn attack early next morning. The 2nd Royal Welch were in reserve for this assault, the main attack being undertaken by the 20th Royal Fusiliers (the Chocolate Soldiers), the 1st Scottish Rifles and the 5th/6th Scottish Rifles. It was made very clear by General Haig, General Rawlinson, by Division and by Brigade that the capture of High Wood was of vital importance. As he briefed his officers of the 2nd Royal Welch, Colonel Crawshay was not optimistic and suggested that if the Battalion was called forward in support it would be decimated. The Battalion handed over to its relief and then took shelter in the many shell holes at the north end of Happy Valley, an attractive target for the German artillery. Zero hour for the High Wood attack was 3.30 am. From then on the Battalion was under continuous enemy fire and it was around mid-morning during one of these bombardments that Graves was very badly wounded by splinters from a large calibre shell. The battalion had moved close to the village cemetery and amongst the less dangerous wounds was one over Graves' eye caused by a chip of marble from one of the headstones in Bazentin cemetery, but the remaining wounds through the shoulder, chest and thigh were very serious indeed.

At the north end of Mametz Wood the British had taken over a former German Dressing Station, to which Graves was taken. Such were his wounds that he was not expected to live and was therefore placed on a stretcher in a corner where he remained unconscious for 24 hours - but when the orderlies were clearing away the dead next morning, 21 July, he was found to be breathing and was taken by ambulance to the Field Hospital at Heilly. By 24 July (Graves's twenty-first birthday) he was on the way to a military hospital in Rouen and then on to England a few days later where he was installed in Queen Alexandra's hospital in Highgate, north London. As far as the regiment was concerned he had died of his wounds and his name appeared in the

Bazentin-Le-Petit communal cemetery and extension. On 20 July 1916, the British front line ran approximately along the sky-line in this view. Robert Graves, serving with the 2nd Royal Welch Fusiliers, was very badly wounded that day by fragments of a shell that fell in the civilian cemetery. He was taken to a Regimental Aid Post in a small quarry just behind the camera position, then to a former German aid post in Mametz Wood.

long casualty list issued after the battle for High Wood on 20 July.

Sassoon, serving with the 1st Royal Welch transport at Dernancourt, was given the news of his friend's death on 21 July, but two days later he himself was taken ill with fever and sent to the New Zealand Hospital in Amiens. (While there he wrote 'To His Dead Body', referring to the news of Graves's death; it was a fortnight before he learned from Eddie Marsh of his survival, by which time Graves was back in hospital in London.) The bad news continued, for at the end of the month he learned that another of his valued army friends, Marcus Goodall ('Allgood' in *Memoirs of an Infantry Officer*), had died of wounds on 14 July. By 2 August Sassoon was back in England recuperating at No. 3 Southern General Hospital in Somerville College, Oxford.

A corridor ward on a hospital train. A hospital train might consist of up to 17 corridor-type railway carriages, adapted for stretchers to be taken on board easily. In addition to nursing sisters, the train would carry some 50 male orderlies, nurses, cooks etc. The last coach in the train was used as an isolation ward for any infectious disease cases. Robert Graves began his journey back to hospital in England by train after being severely wounded in July 1916.

Even before Graves was wounded it was clear that the battle for High Wood was not going well. Casualties in the Scottish Rifles were mounting rapidly and the position of the 20th Royal Fusiliers was even worse, for quite early on the Commanding Officer had been wounded and left the wood for the dressing station; shortly afterwards the last officer casualty of the 20th Royal Fusiliers, Lieutenant Wallwork, was killed.

The order that Colonel Crawshay had dreaded now came through - to move forward to the wood. Weakened by casualties, the 2nd Royal Welch set off with determination along the road towards Longueval via Crucifix Corner and then down to the south-eastern face of High Wood. The battalion pushed on into the shell-damaged trees, appalled by the sight of the many dead and the wounded who awaited evacuation. In the space of an hour the battalion had retrieved the whole situation, overrunning the various strong points and then finally the whole wood. At nightfall, however, a German counter attack broke through the shattered remnants of the 20th Royal Fusiliers and although the attackers were eventually held, the northern part of High

Wood remained in enemy hands. The wood was held by the Germans until 15 September 1916, when the 47th (London) Division finally took it, with heavy casualties. It had taken two months and untold casualties among several Divisions to clear High Wood (in retrospect, making the efforts of the 38th (Welsh) Division in clearing Mametz Wood within five days appear very creditable).

Two years later the 2nd Royal Welch were back here again; as they advanced through both Mametz Wood and High Wood in August 1918, several officers took the opportunity to explore the two woods, this time in comparative safety.

Remarkably, Graves began to recover from his near-mortal wounds - but as he did so he became aware of various repercussions over his supposed death. One embarrassment was that his pay ceased and the Army bankers refused to honour his cheques. There were flattering letters of sympathy to be answered, and a letter had to go to The Times, explaining that he was not dead but in hospital recovering from his wounds. Letters to the Graves family from his commanding officer, his batman and from Robert himself in hospital confused them with contradictory assertions; one letter that appealed to Graves's sardonic sense of humour was a flattering letter of condolence from his C.O., with whom he had not been on particularly good terms.

Two months later he wrote what he called 'a silly thing', a poem called 'Died of Wounds' in which the lines of carefully varying length were laid out to form the shape of a funeral urn. It turns on the fact that he was pronounced dead on his 21st birthday which, he claimed, excused him from becoming an adult - Time could 'never make a man of me/For I lie dead in Picardy'. It was a particularly cruel twist of fate that at the end of his very long life Graves - like others who fought in the First World War - believed himself back in the front line, a state of mind in the 1970s and 1980s that remained with him for longer than the actual period of his experiences in France over sixty years earlier.

By 26 August 1916 he was fit enough to travel to Harlech, Sassoon following him there three days later. On 11 September both left for Sassoon's country home at Weirleigh in Kent, Graves spending just over a week with Sassoon and his mother. It was during this visit that Graves was disturbed one night by Sassoon's mother and her desperate and noisy attempts to contact the spirit of her dead son Hamo; preferring dramatic anecdote to discreet reticence, he chose to describe the incident (without naming the family) in *Goodbye to All That*, deeply upsetting Sassoon when the book appeared in 1929 with this frank invasion of privacy between friends.

By now both men were in a state of acute nervous tension, misery and anger over the way the war was being managed. Sassoon's poems dating from August 1916 are savage in their sarcasm: 'The One-Legged Man' and 'The Hero' for example, express the images that lodged in his mind as well as how he perceived the prevailing civilian attitudes to the war. The exception from this period is 'The Death-Bed', which is a memory of the hospital in Amiens. Its rich and highly-coloured images of a dying soldier's ebbing and fading mind, as Death comes inexorably closer, are lyrical and atmospheric; the actual scene that he witnessed must have evoked the deaths of many friends lost in the past six months.

Out in France things had not gone well for the 1st Royal Welch, as Graves and Sassoon learned from the long Casualty Lists in the newspapers. Neither High Wood nor Delville Wood were fully cleared of the enemy. On 27 August the 1st Royal Welch were ordered to bomb down a particular trench near Delville Wood in an attempt to clear the sector. (Sassoon's 'Fernby', 2nd-Lieutenant Newton, distinguished himself here.) This was achieved, with heavy casualties, and later they consolidated their gains, taking sixty prisoners. During a violent bombardment two days later, a direct hit on the battalion's Aid Post obliterated everything and everyone in it except the Medical Officer, Sassoon's friend, Lieutenant Kelsey Fry. Completely untouched but suffering from severe shell-shock, he was given a morphine injection and sent off to the Field Ambulance.

LIEUTENANT W. KELSEY FRY, MC, RAMC

Dr.W. Kelsey Fry, born in 1889, was the popular Medical Officer for the 1st Royal Welch who served with Graves and Sassoon; in *Goodbye to All That* Graves describes him as being a throat specialist in civil life. Concerned that some wounded men were dying unnecessarily through choking on the tongue going backwards into his throat, he conducted an experiment: on the way to the Dressing Station, he walked in front of the wounded man allowing the soldier to lean forward on to him. The procedure was successful, but there was always the danger that an R.A.M.C. orderly would instruct the casualty to lie down on a stretcher – in which case the man could then die of a throat obstruction, a matter of continuing concern to the doctor. Twice wounded, Kelsey Fry returned to the Regimental Depot and was then seconded to Queen's Hospital in Sidcup, Kent, where he specialised in facial surgery and treatment for injuries to the jaw. Later he worked with the distinguished surgeon Sir Harold Gillies CBE, where his war experiences enabled him to become an expert in plastic surgery relating to jaw and facial injuries. He was later knighted, and died in 1963. (The hospital retains its historic links with this pioneering work, in the form of an archive of facial injury records from the First World War.)

The loss of life among Graves's and Sassoon's friends had been high: Captain Edmund Dadd had been killed and his brother Julian seriously wounded in the throat. The horrendous nature of this battle and the sights he had seen were always with Julian Dadd and he suffered mentally for years after the war, perhaps a contributory factor in his untimely death in 1937.

Second Lieutenant Newton had been badly wounded too, both officers being taken to a base hospital at Rouen where Newton succumbed to his wounds on the 15th September.

SECOND LIEUTENANT VIVIAN FREDERIC NEWTON

In his fictionalised memoirs, Sassoon gave him the fictional name of 'Fernby'. After passing out at Sandhurst in October 1915 Newton was commissioned into the Royal Welch Fusiliers and in May 1916 joined the Regiment's 1st Battalion, where he immediately impressed his Commanding Officer, Lieutenant-Colonel Stockwell. Seriously wounded near Delville Wood on 3rd September 1916, he was taken to a military hospital at Rouen, where he eventually died of his wounds on 15 September, aged 19. Stockwell wrote to the mother of this only child: 'A charming boy - always keen and full of pluck; so much so that I especially selected him to go to the grenadier company, the picked company of the battalion. He did some splendid work with the bombs on 26-27 August 1916 (the attack on Delville Wood) in some very severe fighting, and on the day he was wounded he was in command of the battalion bombers. His loss will be felt by all of us who were his brother-officers as he was universally liked because of his straightness and keenness'.

Convalescent leave over, Graves reported to the Regiment at Litherland in the middle of November where he was followed early in December by Sassoon, both awaiting examination by a Medical Board. They were to have almost six weeks together before Graves was warned for overseas service. Officers from the camp were given honorary membership of the attractive and well-established Formby Golf Club; Sassoon played golf there with his friend Second Lieutenant R.R.

Brocklebank and occasionally with Graves, who annoyed Sassoon by not taking the game seriously enough.

During this time Julian Dadd came to stay in Liverpool for a night. Speaking in a whisper because of his throat wound, he told Sassoon about the terrible fighting at Ginchy in September; Sassoon wrote about this visit in his poem 'A Whispered Tale'. There were other officers of the 1st Royal Welch in the barracks at that time too: Lieutenant E. L. Orme, Lieutenant J. B. P. Adams, Sassoon's close friend, Second Lieutenant 'Bobbie' Hanmer, newly commissioned Second Lieutenant A.M. Syrett, an energetic piano player fresh from training with the Artists Rifles, and Sassoon's nineteen year-old golfing partner, Second Lieutenant R.R. Brocklebank, all destined to be killed or wounded within the next five months.

SECOND LIEUTENANT ROBERT H. HANMER – 'BOBBIE'

Sassoon had known the Hanmer family in 1913, and indeed became deeply attached to 'Bobbie' – although he seems to have recognised that it would be wise to conceal the emotional depth of the attachment. In two introspective diary entries in April 1916, he refers to his experiences and his losses: 'Now I've known love for Bobbie and Tommy [David Thomas] ...' and, a week later, 'Tommy dead; and Bobbie Hanmer at Salonika; I can't keep them clear in memory; they fade, with their bright hair and happy eyes'. Early in 1916 he became engaged to Hanmer's sister Dorothy, but the engagement seems to have been a way of remaining close to her brother and it was

Formby Golf Club and links. Siegfried Sassoon and Robert Graves played golf here when stationed at nearby Litherland Camp.

broken off a few months later; his diary for July 1916 records:
' ... the Hanmer engagement idea was a ghastly blunder - it wouldn't work at all. That charming girl who writes to me so often would never be happy with me. It was my love for Bobbie that led me to that mistake'.

On 22 January 1917 Graves set off once again, clearly not fully fit but impatient to return to France, and rejoined the 2nd Royal Welch on 26 January. Indeed, the remarks of the President of the Medical Board in December 1916, made it clear that Graves could quite easily have been granted several more months of home service. In the light of what happened a few months later the doctors were obviously right, but chose to fall in with Graves's keenness to return to his friends, the Board's decision probably being influenced by recent events on the Somme. When Sassoon appeared for medical assessment in the same month, he was granted another month's service at home.

The final battles of the Somme campaign had only recently finished. Both sides were re-grouping and, in the case of the British, there was an urgent need for reinforcements to replace their heavy casualties. It was only to be expected that the cases of wounded officers and men would be reviewed to see if they could quickly be sent back to their units. The German Army had also suffered heavily in those battles and their urgent need was to shorten their line and conserve man-power. This they did, in February-March 1917, through a carefully managed fighting retreat to a series of almost impregnable defences called the Hindenburg Line. Sassoon was to experience the quality of this dreaded defence line a few months later.

The British had recently taken over from the French 17th Division in the Cléry-sur-Somme zone; on arrival, the 2nd Royal Welch were surprised to see a Paris bus which turned out to be a carrier pigeon loft. The Battalion's position was known as Cléry Left although the village itself, now no more than a mass of shell craters, was almost unidentifiable. From the high ground that they occupied, facing the German lines to the east, they could clearly see the wooded hill of Mont St. Quentin and Péronne beyond.

The day before Graves joined the battalion, the Commanding Officer, 'Tibs' Crawshay, had been wounded in his arm and side by a German sniper while out on patrol with Dr. Dunn, the Battalion Medical Officer. They had been inspecting the wire in No Man's Land when they became silhouetted against the sky even though it was quite dark. Because of his wounds he was not to return to the battalion, Lieutenant-Colonel W.B. Garnett taking over command the following

114

Cléry, two views. Above, the ruined refinery, below, the devasted
landscape by the end of the war.
Graves was here in March 1917 with the 2nd Royal Welch Fusiliers.

The valley of the Somme at Cléry, a painting dated September 1916. Later, the British Army took over from the French 17th Division here.

month. After the war, Colonel Crawshay's wounds necessitated repeated medical attention until he died in 1937.

Graves was allocated to the Headquarters Company in the rear echelon, which meant that he was in charge of the Battalion specialists - cooks, pioneers, drivers etc., a fortunate employment in view of his poor health. He joined the 2nd Royal Welch at the beginning of an exceptionally cold spell, with frozen snow everywhere: during the following weeks temperatures of 15 degrees of frost were common and the ground was often frozen to a depth of 16 inches. Coke for the fires was scarce - and even when it was obtainable there were cases of coke-fume poisoning where the troops had slept in badly ventilated dug-outs. There were no trees left, but a few remaining saplings had been dug out of the ground and their roots used in an attempt to make a small fire. Even the wooden crosses on isolated graves had been taken. Unsurprisingly, considering the conditions the men had to endure out in the open, the numbers at the Battalion's sick parade began to increase and in one two-day period a total of nearly 200 reported sick with colds, trench fever and influenza. One officer was sent off to hospital with measles.

LETTER-POEMS

Graves and Sassoon (and, on at least one occasion, Robert Nichols) wrote several long letter-poems to each other about the war, reflecting their personal attitudes and hopes for the future. In May 1916 Sassoon wrote 'A Letter Home (to Robert Graves)' at the Army School in Flixécourt, explaining how he had 'seen/Soldier David dressed in green...' - the lovely

116

The ruined church at Frise, September 1916. Robert Graves and the 2nd Royal Welch were here in February 1917, before he was taken ill and sent back to England.

The rebuilt church at Frise.

landscape far behind the lines had reminded him of their young friend David Thomas and he had seen him as a kind of mystic figure of Nature in the woodland.

Graves responded with 'Familiar Letter to Siegfried Sassoon (*From Bivouacs at Mametz Wood, July 13th, 1916*)', retracing their conversation after their unexpected meeting near Fricourt when they passed the time 'Plotting such marvellous journeys there/For golden-houred 'Après-la-guerre'...'. The poem ranges over the places that they planned to visit together when the longed-for peace arrived - North Wales first of all, his treasured second home, before sailing off to explore the Caucasus and the original home of the Sassoons in Baghdad, then 'Bitlis and Mush will know our faces,/Tiflis and Tomsk, and all such places' followed by 'the Tartars of Thibet/Hobnobbing with the Chungs and Mings,/And doing wild, tremendous things/In free adventure, quest and fight,/And God! what poetry we'll write!'

When Robert Nichols wrote to Graves in the bitter winter of 1916-17 about the delights of rural life and picking cherries, Graves replied from the equally fierce cold at Frise, on the Somme, `Here by a snow-bound river/In scrapen holes we

117

shiver,/And like old bitterns we/Boom to you plaintively'.

Later, when Sassoon was in hospital in London in July 1918, he wrote his poetic 'Letter to Robert Graves', a tense, unhappy ramble through all the circumstances that are making him unhappy and including some invented portmanteau words to describe his emotional state (for example, 'Sleeplessexasperuicide') as well as references to people in his life ('Jolly Otterleen' for Lady Ottoline Morrell, and his revered psychiatric doctor, W. H. R. Rivers). The poem was first published, without permission and in a garbled form, in *Goodbye to All That*: another cause for a major rift between the two created by the book's publication.

Division decided that it needed to learn what was taking place on the German side of the lines. Corps then took up the idea and plans were drawn up for the seizure of Hertzfeldt trench, about a mile south of Bouchavesnes village and 500 yards to the west of the Péronne – Bapaume main road. Conferences were held to discuss the details, involving Graves at one stage when asked to deputise. Discussions continued with those having to make the attack, every one of whom was doubtful of any success being possible. Eventually, and to the Royal Welch's relief, the whole idea was abandoned after three weeks of planning, not least because the 18th Middlesex (the Pioneer battalion), ordered to excavate the required communication trenches, pointed out that the heavy frost had made the ground absolutely impossible to dig.

By the beginning of March 1917 the 2nd Royal Welch were in the Suzanne and Frise area beside the River Somme, still suffering intensely cold conditions, but by 11 March they had reached Corbie and their time on the Somme battlefield was almost over. The toll over the months was some 200 of the battalion 'buried and unburied'. By this time Graves felt exhausted. The Battalion doctor diagnosed bronchitis; he was sent to hospital in Rouen and eventually to Somerville College in Oxford, now converted to a hospital.

The War Diary entry for the Battalion dated 12 March 1917 bore the entry 'Capt. R. von R. Graves to England sick and struck off strength of the Battalion'. The next day it included an entry recording the fact that Second Lieutenant Sassoon had joined the Battalion from Base. Preparations for a battalion move north to Arras would soon begin.

Chapter Six

1917

On 27th January 1917 Sassoon was passed fit for France. After a week on leave at home he left on a draft for France and reached the Infantry Base Depot in Rouen on 16 February - where he went down with German measles. After ten days, however, he was fit again, awaiting instructions to join the 2nd Royal Welch; despite an initial preference for the 1st Royal Welch he was soon at ease in the 2nd battalion and only a few weeks later was sorry to leave them. Midnight on 11 March found Sassoon in Corbie, spending an uncomfortable night sleeping on the Field Ambulance floor. Next day he reported to the Battalion in the Rest camp at Chipilly, where the 2nd Royal Welch was now part of Lieutenant-General Sir Ivor Maxse's XVIII Corps under General Sir Edmund Allenby's Third Army. Known as Camp 13, it lay on low ground far from any amenities, forcing the troops to spend dismal evenings in its numerous cold and draughty huts. Life was more agreeable for officers, however, and for nearly three weeks Sassoon, without formal duties, enjoyed trips to Heilly and other places familiar from past visits with friends in the Royal Welch, including visits to Amiens to enjoy splendid meals at the Godbert restaurant.

The Church at Corbie. Sassoon was in camp near here in March-April 1917 with the 2nd Royal Welch, joining them on 13 March. Graves was struck off the battalion's strength the previous day because of illness and sent back to England.

Orders to move came through by 1 April and the Battalion moved off next day to Corbie to begin the long march to the Arras front. Some officers had already been taken out of the Battalion to form a reserve, but Sassoon joined B Company under Captain W. W. Kirkby. (Sassoon's fictional 'Leake').

Early in 1917 the French artilleryman General Robert Nivelle devised a plan which he promised would ensure an Allied victory in a matter of days and in particular

Amiens Cathedral. The magnificent Gothic cathedral greatly impressed Sassoon when he visited it in March 1917, just before leaving for the Arras front with the 2nd RWF. Despite enemy bombardment the cathedral suffered only slight damage during hostilities. The priceless stained-glass windows had been removed by firemen from the Paris brigade, and the sandbag defences in front of the building were augmented by many more inside.

managed to persuade the British Government that his ideas would be effective. This involved the French in a main attack on the Chemin des Dames front, east of Soissons, with a secondary French Army offensive taking place to the west of that town. The British were given a subsidiary role, attacking on a front stretching north from Bapaume to Arras, to involve the First, Third and Fourth Armies. Later, the strategically significant Vimy Ridge area north of Arras was to be added to the British plans. In the event, the French Army attacks failed with heavy casualties, and in the subsequent loss of morale, many of their men refused to go on fighting. The British had much greater success, the Canadian Corps taking Vimy Ridge whilst British troops penetrated the notorious Hindenburg Line south of Arras. In what was perhaps the most savage infantry battle of the whole war, casualties were heavy: calculated on a daily basis – over 4,000 a day – they exceeded those of either the Somme or Passchendaele battles. With the

Amiens, the former Belfort Hotel (now the Carlton). Sassoon stayed overnight here in March 1917, after an expensive meal with friends at the Godbert restaurant. He occupied one of the balcony bedrooms from which he could see the station opposite, and the dim lights of the town.

French Army temporarily weakened by mutinies, the British were forced to continue their pressure on the German defences longer than they would have wished, sustaining the campaign until 15 May when, under great pressure, Nivelle was finally forced to resign his command.

By 3 April the 2nd Royal Welch were on the march, their route taking them along the Amiens road to Doullens and then via Lucheux and Saulty to Basseux which they reached on Easter Sunday 8 April 1917. Although still in the Third Army, they had now left Maxse's XVIII Corps, which was not to take an active part in the forthcoming Arras battles. The Battalion, now barely 300 strong, was to be in VII Corps under Lieutenant-General Sir Thomas Snow.

Lieutenant-General Sir Thomas Snow, commanding officer of the VII Corps under whom the 2nd RWF fought at Arras in 1917.

SIR IVOR MAXSE

This outstanding general was renowned for his emphasis on training, often to the annoyance of tired troops, including the 2nd Royal Welch. It was apparently Sir Ivor's practice when visiting units under his command to pose the question: 'I'm a machine-gun, what would you do?' On one occasion an infantryman responded promptly: 'I'm a 5.9 howitzer, what would you do, General?'

Going along the road to Doullens, the battalion had been called to attention as it marched past its former Corps Commander and its Divisional Commander. The Commanding Officer of the 2nd Royal Welch, Lieutenant-Colonel Garnett (Sassoon's fictional 'Easby') saluted the General while still mounted on his charger. Garnett's unintentional discourtesy in remaining on his horse brought forth a storm of criticism from the General, along with adverse comments on the march discipline of his Battalion as it had passed by him in the wet snow. During this public denunciation one of the causes of the General's irritation – the untidy field-cookers laden with brooms and the cooks' kit – went on steadily trundling past, belching smoke from their chimneys and cooking the troops' dinners along the way.

Lieutenant-Colonel W.B. Garnett who commanded the 2nd RWF when Sassoon was serving with the battalion in April 1917, during the Battle of Arras. The colonel's son, Lieutenant J.B. Garnett, was killed in 1940 whilst in action with the 1st battalion and is buried in France, at Saint Floris, near the place where Sassoon was wounded in 1918.

MEETING THE CORPS COMMANDER

This encounter with Maxse may have inspired what is probably Sassoon's best-known poem, 'The General': referring to two old soldiers on their way up to Arras, it records the General's cheery greeting ('Good-morning, good-morning' the General said ...') and the soldiers' muttered approval – but by the end, the men that he greeted are 'most of'em dead'. It is a very short poem: the final line, set separately from the first six ('But he did for them both by his plan of attack') is a far more incisive indictment of military staff-work and generalship than could have been achieved in a longer piece.

When the Battle of Arras began at 5.30 am on 9 April 1917 the 2nd Royal Welch were at Basseux, about two miles from the city, awaiting instructions to move forward. By 12 April Sassoon was with his battalion at St.Martin-Cojeul, now only about a mile from the partially captured Hindenburg Line, awaiting orders in a cold and cramped dug-out with his friends Kirkby, Casson and Evans.

The formidable defences of the Hindenburg Line near St. Martin-Cojeul, much of it built by Russian prisoners, were of impressive construction: two rows of trenches about 200 yards apart, well

Sassoon at the Battle of Arras 1917, showing the sector stretching from Vimy Ridge in the north to Fontaine-lés-Croisilles (where Sassoon lost many friends) in the south. The poet Ivor Gurney, serving with the 2nd/5th Glosters, was at Wailly, South west of Arras during the battle, and later at Guémappe, helping to clear the battlefield.

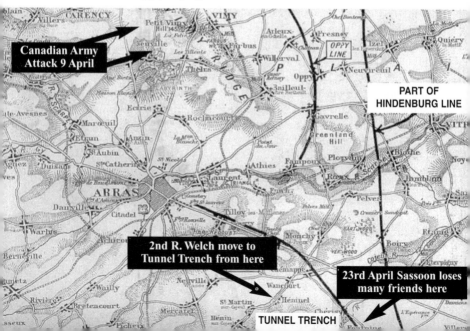

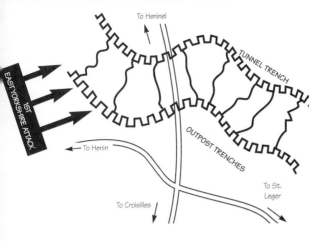

To Heninel

TUNNEL TRENCH

1ST EAST YORKSHIRE ATTACK

OUTPOST TRENCHES

To Henin

To Croisilles

To St. Leger

Arras, 9 April 1917. The Hindenburg Line, Tunnel Trench. Showing the area in which the 2nd RWF were in action and the Tunnel Trench sector where Sassoon was wounded on 16th April 1917. The 1st East Yorks. were the only troops to breach the Hindenburg Line on 9 April, though at a cost of 287 casualties.

protected by barbed wire, each trench wide enough to stop any advance by British tanks. The front trench, about 10 feet deep, was protected by concrete machine-gun nests at roughly 50-yard intervals. The support line, known to the British as Tunnel Trench, was linked by communication trenches to the front line. Underneath the support trench the Germans had built a huge accommodation tunnel, two miles long and about 40 feet below ground, with rooms of various sizes and full height.

The initial responsibility for breaching the Hindenburg Line at this point on 9 April was given to the 1st East Yorkshires. The main bombardment here began at 7.30 am on a bitterly cold morning with snow on the ground, but it was not until mid-afternoon, under cover of another barrage, that the East Yorks. went forward. Within 25 minutes

A German shelter or tunnel trench under construction showing the corrugated iron sheeting used to support the roof.

An Officer Cadet Training Unit on parade at an Oxford College. Robert Graves was a Temporary Instructor with No. 4 Officer Cadet battalion in Wadham College in 1917. Note the white cap bands which indicate Officer Cadet status.

the Battalion had captured the outer line of the Hindenburg defences, the first British troops to do so. Some platoons made for the support trenches but they were stubbornly held by the German defenders and they had to fall back. Unfortunately the battalion's flanks could not be secured by the 15th Durhams and the 9th King's Own Yorkshire Light Infantry, and the East Yorkshires were therefore isolated. Next day the inevitable enemy counter attack was driven off with casualties on both sides, but eventually the East Yorkshires could no longer hold their position and had to withdraw to their original starting point.

By 12 April, however, the 18th Manchesters had forced the German defenders to give up a considerable length of the Hindenburg Line, and the East Yorkshires' objectives now fell into British hands. A number of wounded British soldiers were discovered in the deep shelters, captured in the German counter-attack against the East Yorkshires. Their captors had treated them well, and indeed they were given hot coffee just before the Germans retreated. The next orders were for the 5th Scottish Rifles with the 1st Scottish Rifles to advance as far as a sunken road near Fontaine-lès-Croisilles, bombing down the Hindenburg line and at the same time advancing over open ground.

Early on Saturday 14 April the 5th Scottish Rifles went into the attack just east of St. Martin-Cojeul where, despite failing to gain their objective, they captured some 1000 yards of enemy ground and 700 German prisoners. The 219 British casualties included Company

Sergeant Major J. Erskine, who as a sergeant had won the Victoria Cross in June 1916 at the Red Dragon Crater, Givenchy. Late that night the battalion handed over to the 20th Royal Fusiliers. Meanwhile, the 1st Scottish Rifles, bombing down the Hindenburg Line trenches, could only advance 150 yards whilst their attack over open ground gained only 100 yards.

It was now time for the 2nd Royal Welch to join in the fighting. Late on 15 April the Battalion set off in the dark from the ruins of St.Martin-Cojeul to take over part of the Tunnel Trench line in support of the 1st Scottish Rifles. The two guides from the 13th Northumberland Fusiliers set off with confidence in a sector now completely devoid of any landmarks, to lead the heavily laden Royal Welch to their new positions. Lightly equipped, they set off at great speed with the Battalion struggling to keep up behind them and it soon became obvious that the guides were completely lost.

With his usual impulsive independence Sassoon left his company and set off on his own, luckily finding a party of Royal Engineers who were able to give him directions. They were in the midst of British and German dead, many from the fighting of April 9 and 10 – as Sassoon recorded in his diary, 'the most ghastly sights ... beyond description'. In later months, these sights would feed through directly and indirectly into a number of poems of bitter intensity.

After seeing his company (now down to eighty men) in position, and with the possibility of having to attack along the tunnel as far as a barrier or 'stop', he decided to make a reconnaissance along the ill-lit tunnel trench – a distance of some 900 yards. It was a dreadful place, with German and British dead awaiting burial, a place of latrine smells and mud mixed in with refuse of every description. Next morning, after taking charge of a fatigue party carrying trench mortar bombs to the front line, he was told to take command of a Royal Welch bombing party of 100 men who would act as a reserve for the 1st Scottish Rifles.

The failure of the Scottish Rifles' attacks the previous Saturday was now to be redeemed and they were ordered to bomb down the two Hindenburg Line trenches again on 16 April, to recover lost ground; zero hour was 3 am. After a wait of three hours in the Hindenburg Line tunnel on April 16, Sassoon was suddenly ordered to take 25 of his Royal Welch bombers, including his platoon sergeant (the invaluable Sergeant Baldwin), to help men of the Scottish Rifles who were in trouble in one of the Hindenburg Line trenches. To his relief, help was needed above ground and not in the gruesome tunnel. After running out of bombs the Scottish Rifles were slowly being driven back, but with the aid of Sassoon and his party the German attack was held and the lost ground regained. Whilst his men were consolidating he went exploring down a side trench – and peered over the trench parapet during a lull in the enemy machine-gun fire. It was a foolish move, for he was immediately seen by a sniper and hit in the shoulder by a rifle bullet. Faint with shock, he was quickly discovered by Sergeant Baldwin leaning against the trench wall and led back to the main trench.

Shortly after this the Scottish Rifles were recalled and the rest of the 2nd Royal Welch took over. As the initial successes were not being repeated, a dissatisfied Field Marshal Haig now postponed all attacks for seven days until the next stage in the Arras offensive, on 23 April. It proved to be a terrible battle, and brought the tragic death and wounding of many of Sassoon's friends.

After just four hours in action, Sassoon left the trenches to get treatment for his wound, going down into the tunnel to the Regimental Aid Post. From there he walked to Henin Dressing Station where Private Mansfield, his servant, was waiting to assist him and then on to Boyelles, where he arrived, not surprisingly, tired and weary. This was the end of his connection with the 2nd Royal Welch, regular army battalions and, temporarily, his service under its Army Commander, General Allenby. It had lasted just 36 days. His participation in the Battle of Arras was even briefer, a mere five days, but his experiences during those days remained vivid in his mind for the rest of his life.

After a short time at the Casualty Clearing Station Sassoon was put on a Red Cross train and reached a tented hospital at Camières late next day (17 April). Forty-eight hours later he was on the move again, in a hospital ship crossing the Channel, and reached a Denmark Hill military hospital in London on 20 April.

DANGER AT SEA

Had Sassoon known it, March-April 1917 was a particularly hazardous time for hospital ships. In March the Union Castle liner S.S *Glenart Castle* was torpedoed by UC56 with the loss of 168 lives, including the Master, while later in that month another hospital ship, the S.S. *Gloucester Castle*, was lost through enemy action. Two days before Sassoon crossed the Channel two more hospital ships were lost, both carrying casualties from the Arras battles and both sailing to Southampton. The former Midland Railway Company ferry, the S.S. *Donegal*, was torpedoed by UC 21 south of Spithead and the Booth Lines' S.S. *Lanfranc* by UB40 some 42 miles out from Le Havre. In the War Crimes trials in 1921 a U-Boat commander was tried for his part in sinking a hospital ship but was acquitted, apparently on the grounds that the ship was not maintaining a straight heading, as expected of a hospital ship, but following a zig-zag course like an ordinary merchantman.

Slowly news of the Battle of Arras came through to Sassoon. The 2nd Royal Welch had taken part in yet another attack towards Fontaine-lès-Croisilles in the early dawn of 23 April, managing to get within 300 yards of the objective before being held up. Support came at one stage in the form of a British tank driving parallel to the front line and knocking out the German machine-gun emplacements: but the Royal Welch suffered a heavy toll, for the casualties included some 120 Other Ranks and thirteen officers, among them Sassoon's friend Bobbie Hanmer.

The Arras battles took a similar toll on the 1st Royal Welch and among the 13 officers and 175 other rank casualties were Sassoon's friends Second Lieutenants Syrett and Brocklebank (his former golfing partner) and the Padre, Captain the Hon. M. Peel.

VISIT NO. 4: TUNNEL TRENCH, near ARRAS

Leaving Arras via Beaurains, continue through Neuville-Vitasse on the **D 5** (where Sassoon received some trench experience with the Canadians) and continue south on the same road to Henin-sur-Cojeul. Turn left here on to the **D 33** at the crossroads in the village. The road takes you under the motorway and into Heninel; turn to the right at the cross-roads, with its CWGC cemetery signs, including Heninel-Croisilles Road. Following this name, bear right at the fork after 500 yards, go up the hill and continue to the cemetery on the left.

There is no trace of the trench itself but its approximate location is easy to find since the present-day Heninel-Croisilles Road British Cemetery marks part of Tunnel Trench and the area in which Sassoon was in action when he was wounded in April 1917. Continuing past the cemetery up the slight rise, it is possible to see the remains of some of the fortifications from that period.

The cemetery contains some Scottish Rifles graves, from the unit that Sassoon went to help. There are also graves of men from the 1st East Yorks, the 20th Royal Fusiliers, 5th Scottish Rifles and the 2nd Royal Welch Fusiliers.

Back in England, Graves was in hospital in Oxford at this time, first in Somerville College and then, having recovered from bronchitis, in Wadham College as a Temporary Instructor with No. 4 Officer Cadet battalion. He appreciated the comforts of life here, treated as a senior member of the college hierarchy with 'access to the famous brown sherry'. One of his cadet students recorded later that Graves was clearly affected by shell-shock, and no doubt he particularly appreciated his frequent week-end visits to Lady Ottoline Morrell's house at Garsington, a few miles away from Oxford. His health deteriorated, however and, after fainting and hurting his head, he was despatched first to hospital once more and then, early in June, to Osborne House, Isle of Wight. Queen Victoria's house on the island had become a convalescent home for officers. It was during the period in hospital before this convalescence that Graves fell in love with a girl for the first time in his life – with one of the nurses, a professional pianist in peace-time; hitherto his emotional attachments had been a hero-worshipping intensity of concentration on an idealised male figure, who in most cases did not return his depth of feeling.

While Graves was convalescing in Osborne House, Sassoon was getting into complicated waters. The process that began when he first saw action, and translated it into more powerful poetry which reflected his experiences in and around the front line along the Western Front, was developing further. Through his friendships in London literary and intellectual life he fell under the influence of Bertrand Russell and others who added to his own dissatisfaction with the war: not only the terrible sights in the front line, particularly around Arras in April 1917, but the apparent uselessness of the heavy losses and what he saw as a distortion of the original war aims.

In March 1917 he had written (in 'Return') of the men who remained, dead, on the battlefield while he returned alive from it; 'The Rear-Guard', written in hospital late in April (a few days after being wounded in the Hindenburg Line) is a powerful evocation of the atmosphere deep underground: he describes his exploration along a tunnel, stopping to ask a sleeping man to guide him, getting no answer – and finding himself talking to a corpse, the dead man's face still full of the agony of his wounding and death. The writer 'with sweat of horror in his hair' returns to the dawn light overhead, 'unloading hell behind him step by step'. He returned to the theme the next day, with 'To The Warmongers', with its opening line, 'I'm back again from hell', description of 'young faces bleared with blood,/Sucked down into the mud' and the ending, 'For I have watched them die'.

Héninel-Croisilles Cemetery. The front of the cemetery wall marks the location of Tunnel Trench in April 1917. The action in which Sassoon was wounded probably took place somewhere near here, along the road visible in the photograph. The cemetery contains graves of men of 1st East Yorks. 20th Royal Fusiliers ('The Chocolate Soldiers'), Royal Welch Fusiliers and Scottish Rifles. The latter belonged to the battalion which Sassoon was sent to assist in their attack. Eleven German soldiers are also buried here.

It was during this period in hospital that he wrote 'The General', with its reference to the men who 'slogged up to Arras with rifle and pack.' and the deadly final line that expresses Sassoon's attitude, seeing the battle specifically from the men's point of view. It may have been unfair to pin down the precise responsibility in this way, but it

South of Arras, Tunnel Trench. A recent photograph taken from the 1917 position of one of the Hindenburg Line bunkers (now partially buried), looking towards the rear of the German front line position, with the Cross of Sacrifice in Héninel-Croisilles Road Cemetery just visible in the centre-right. It was here that on 9 April 1917 the 1st East Yorks., despite having broken through the Hindenburg Line, were unable to advance further, without flank support, to capture the German second line close to Tunnel Trench (near the present-day cemetery).

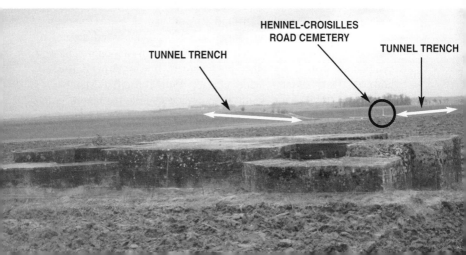

TUNNEL TRENCH

HENINEL-CROISILLES ROAD CEMETERY

TUNNEL TRENCH

undoubtedly expressed the feelings of many front-line soldiers – and Sassoon, whose intellectual courage matched the determined bravery which won him the Military Cross, came to feel increasingly that the war being waged was not the conflict for which he and so many others had enlisted. His sympathies lay with the volunteers and conscripted men rather than with his senior officers who bore the heavy responsibility of command.

In May 1917 Sassoon was convalescing in an old-fashioned country house in Sussex, with an atmosphere that must have reminded him of his childhood but which contrasted uncomfortably with what he now felt about the war. Review notices reached him here about his newly-published anthology, *The Old Huntsman and Other Poems*, a combination of lyrical delight in nature – even in war-ravaged France – and some sad or savage reflections on the war. Reading the reviews, in the quiet and comfortable surroundings of rural England, emphasised to him the shift in his personal commitment: individuals, soldiers or friends who suffered and fought, were far more important than the abstract rights or wrongs of the war. By the time he left the convalescent home he was determined to do something active to utter his protest against the war – neither his whole-hearted front-line service nor the powerful poetry that he was now creating in his anger were enough to arouse public sympathy for the soldier-victims.

His friendships with Bertrand Russell, Lady Ottoline Morrell and her husband, and others in their circle, added to his restlessness and confusion. News of the death of one of his 2nd Battalion friends, Lieutenant E.L. Orme (who was killed in action on 27 May 1917), inspired the bitterness, misery and despair of 'To Any Dead Officer'. It ends: '.... I'm blind with tears,/Staring into the dark. Cheero!/I wish they'd killed you in a decent show'.

This poem is dated 'Mid-June 1917', coinciding with his famous 'Statement' (15 June) in which he expressed his objections to the way in which the war was being prolonged. It was written with the help and support of the Morrells, Bertrand Russell and H.W. Massingham – editor of The Nation, the journal which had published several of Sassoon's poems and which was broader in its approach and sympathies than many other publications. It was through Russell, however, that Sassoon made contact with a pacifist Member of Parliament (H. B. Lees-Smith) who agreed to raise the matter in the House of Commons; Russell was very well aware of Sassoon's value – an officer decorated for his courage and widely known to the public through his poetry.

Litherland Camp in the Great War, Orrell Road main gate guard. A specially posed and interesting photograph of the guard taken in front of the Main Gate Room, with the sentry at his post. The Guard Commander, a sergeant, is flanked by the Duty Bugler and five riflemen and two orderlies. As well as some ceremonial duties, the guard would be responsible for supervising any soldiers in the Guard Room cells (their ventilators project from the roof). Orderlies would be excused sentry duties but would be responsible for bringing meals to the guard and men in the cells.

Sassoon's statement expressed his belief in the distortion of the original British war aims – that the war was now being deliberately prolonged for purposes that were not stated earlier; and that the war was now one 'of aggression and conquest'. His protest was not over the military conduct of the war but against the 'political errors and insincerities' for which he believed the fighting men were being sacrificed. Having drawn it up and considered it carefully, he was unsure of his own nerve in publishing it and suffering the inevitable consequences, including being misunderstood by his fellow officers.

The serious alarm and indecision that he created with this statement continued behind the scenes for some weeks; the strain was intensified during this supposedly quiet time of rest, for before the storm that

Litherland Camp. A modern view of the camp site. The main entrance was probably on the site of the gate visible here, with the Guard Room on the right behind the metal railings.

arose with publication Sassoon's mother had no knowledge of it – he was well aware of his mother's whole-hearted approval of the war, and the calm of his beloved home, Weirleigh, could not relieve his mind. By 4 July, when Sassoon had already overstayed his leave by a week, he was summoned by telegram to go immediately to Litherland Camp. After a day of delay and thought he sent an answer and a copy of the statement to the regiment on 6 July – and, after a second summons, he travelled to Litherland on 13 July.

Two of his most influential literary friends, Eddie Marsh and Robbie Ross, were both thoroughly concerned at the action, while Robert Graves was both astonished and deeply alarmed when the news reached him in Osborne House, on 10 July. He immediately threw himself into what could be described, in later terminology, as 'damage limitation': fearing that Sassoon was running the risk of being 'court-martialled, cashiered and imprisoned', he set to work to persuade senior officers that the statement was the result of 'war-weariness', that Sassoon was a medical problem rather than a rebellious officer and that he should be sent on indefinite leave. (In a letter from hospital, in

Osborne House, Isle of Wight. Queen Victoria's former home was used as a convalescent home for wounded officers. Graves was sent here to recuperate in July 1917. W. GUEST

April, Sassoon had told Graves that he saw hallucinations of corpses on the London streets.)

Graves also sought his own discharge from Osborne, to enable him to deal more effectively with his friend's rash venture, and left the Isle of Wight on 16 July. In *Goodbye to All That* he describes how he went on to Litherland to see his friend's state of mind for himself ('he looked very ill') and discovered that Sassoon had thrown the ribbon of his Military Cross into the River Mersey. The Assistant Adjutant at Litherland, Major McCartney-Filgate, treated the errant junior officer (now a full Lieutenant) with sympathy and invited Sassoon to withdraw his statement – but without success, for Sassoon wished to provoke a Court Martial at which he could explain his motives and determination in public. It was during Sassoon's leave this month that he wrote 'Repression of War Experience',[7] a bitter expression of what the war had done to him and others, the final lines could have been offered as evidence of the horror inflicted on him and so many others:

.... – *quite soft ... they never cease –*
Those whispering guns – O Christ, I want to go out
And screech at them to stop – I'm going crazy;
I'm going stark, staring mad because of the guns.[7]

On 30 July the statement was read out in the House of Commons, followed by its appearance in print in *The Times* the next day (*The Bradford Pioneer* published it on 27 July). However, instead of the summons to a Court Martial that he wished to provoke, the poet was told to book himself into the Adelphi Hotel in Liverpool, to await further instructions. The next step was in line with Robert Graves's aim for his friend in this uncomfortable situation – he was instructed to attend a Medical Board. He tore up the instructions, and the travel warrant that accompanied them. The higher authorities in London were determined to avoid a public scandal and allowed the dissident more time, a calm and patient approach that he found much less easy to deal with.

Graves, in collaboration with Eddie Marsh (Private Secretary to Winston Churchill, Minister of Munitions, and therefore in a position of powerful background influence), urged Sassoon to realise that he would never be sent before a Court Martial and ran the risk of being declared insane and sent to a lunatic asylum. Graves had many powerful arguments on his side, including his own undoubted experience and courage in the front line – and also the complication of a German-sounding name. As he pointed out, the first name 'Siegfried'

[7] The same title was used by Dr. W.H.R. Rivers, soon to be Sassoon's doctor, in a lecture in 1917, and reprinted in his 1920 book *Instinct and the Unconscious.*

was open to misinterpretation in the public mind just as his own middle name, 'von Ranke' had aroused considerable suspicion against him among his fellow-officers. Sassoon, he said, would never be able to achieve the publicity he desired for his anti-war cause.

In the face of this statement (backed by Graves's invented assertion that he was speaking 'on the highest authority'), Sassoon accepted, and attended a Medical Board. In an act of real courage on behalf of his friend, Graves gave evidence despite his own undoubted state of nervous fragility; he broke down in tears three times during the interview, and members of the enquiry felt that he rather than Sassoon should have been object of their investigations. But Sassoon was declared to be suffering from neurasthenia and was referred to Craiglockhart Hospital, on the edge of Edinburgh.

Graves was appointed to escort Sassoon to the hospital when he travelled north on 23 July – but missed the train and followed by a later one.

Chapter Seven

A MEETING OF MINDS

Unlike many of the buildings associated with these two men and their life during the First World War, the main building where Sassoon reported at the end of July 1917, Craiglockhart War Hospital, still survives remarkably unchanged. Having been built as a 'hydro', or spa hotel, in the late nineteenth century, it was taken over for use in the war as increasing numbers of officers and men required treatment for what became known as 'shell-shock'. The official diagnosis was 'neurasthenia', covering a wide range of symptoms for which no physical cause could be established, baffling medical science because no previous pattern of assessment and treatment was known.

Although many men recovered from the symptoms of mental disturbance when withdrawn from the front line and treated with simple rest, regular meals and a quiet atmosphere – most were returned to duty within two or three weeks, without going far from their active units – there were also cases which proved intractable and required hospitalisation back in Great Britain. Even there, doubts were widespread as to how to deal with the mental anguish and its physical consequences caused by the unprecedented experiences of twentieth-century warfare. Prolonged bombardment suffered in immobility in the front lines, the dreadful sights that became everyday hazards, the distress of seeing friends and comrades suffering appalling injuries or death in a variety of inhuman ways – such experiences overcame the best of training and strength of mind, and were reflected in a range of physical and mental ways. (The debate about the nature and treatment of these conditions still continues, many decades later.)

In a famous passage in his *Sherston's Progress*, Sassoon describes the atmosphere in Craiglockhart, which he refers to as 'Slateford'. Calling it 'a live museum of war neuroses', he saw that its real nature became more noticeable by night since that was when the doctors

> ...lost control and the hospital became sepulchral and oppressive with saturations of war experience .... Men muttering uneasily or suddenly crying out in their sleep. Around me was that underworld of dreams haunted by submerged memories of warfare and its intolerable shocks and self-lacerating failures to achieve the impossible ... by night each man was back in his

doomed sector of a horror-stricken Front Line, where the panic and stampede of some ghastly experience was re-enacted among the livid faces of the dead ... In the name of civilization these soldiers had been martyred, and it remained for civilization to prove that their martyrdom wasn't a dirty swindle.

Sassoon's doctor in the midst of this emotional turmoil was the remarkable William Rivers, an anthropologist and psychologist who had studied the ancestor-worshipping and cannibal peoples of New Guinea in his search for an understanding of human feeling and motivation. Sassoon seems to have found him the perfect father-figure; in the fictionalised 'Sherston' memoirs, Rivers is the only person who is given his real name, and throughout the passages that relate to the doctor it is clear that he became the only one on whom Sassoon felt he could really rely to guide him and on whom he could unload his anxieties. Rivers reassured him, questioned him carefully, and brought him to an understanding of himself and his motives. He himself was also acutely aware of his odd position – a doctor, committed to healing, whose job in Craiglockhart Military Hospital was to persuade men back into sound mental health so that they could return to their work of killing.

Amidst the misery of so many minds distorted by war, Sassoon made a notable acquaintance when a hero-worshipping younger officer knocked on his door one day in August 1917, with an armful of copies of *The Old Huntsman* to be signed. This turned out to be Wilfred Owen, then entirely unknown and unpublished, who had been deeply impressed by Sassoon's fierce satirical poems about the war. Further impressed by the older man's sophistication and style, he shyly admitted to being a poet himself, and the two men were soon deep in discussion of the making of poetry: Sassoon, somewhat bored at first

Craiglockhart War Hospital, Edinburgh. Now part of Napier University, the building was used as a hospital for officers with 'neurasthenia'. Sassoon arrived here in July 1917 and met Wilfred Owen soon after. Graves visited Sassoon and also met Owen.

by Owen's timid enthusiasm, urged him to write about his war experience, the events that had brought him to a hospital for neurasthenics. Owen immediately produced work in Sassoon's own style, replacing his own more florid and romantic style but soon moving on to demonstrate his greater mastery of language and technique. Robert Graves was part of this charmed circle within the Craiglockhart world, for on one of his visits to Sassoon, on 13 October 1917, he met Owen, recognised his gifts and added his own encouragement.

A LITERARY COINCIDENCE

The significance of this encounter between the two poets – one famous, innovative and respected, the other entirely unknown, struggling to find his voice – has been much discussed and analysed. At one time, much later, Sassoon expressed mild irritation at being sought out more for his reminiscences and opinions on Owen than for his own work, but he and Graves undoubtedly recognised the newcomer's talents. They were proud to have helped him personally as well as in literary terms. Sassoon was among the first poets to bring forceful realism to war poetry and Owen realised that this was an authentic voice of the real war, disturbing for civilians but welcomed by other soldiers.

The chance circumstances that brought the two men together gave them time to appreciate each other's gifts and to enhance each other's efforts; one of the earliest consequences was Owen's 'Anthem for Doomed Youth', completed with a few touches from Sassoon's pen, but distinctly Owen's own work.

The expedient of despatching Sassoon to a hospital for neurasthenic officers angered him, but achieved its purpose of reducing the effect of his public statement. His potential nuisance-value was considerable, both as an officer and as a figure in literary life – for associated with his undoubted courage came a certain recklessness over the consequences, for others as well as himself. The development of this physical determination can be seen in his younger self, following hounds and riding in local races. Although severely affected by the war, particularly the events around Arras in April 1917, and deeply distressed at the pain, loss of life and suffering of men in his care, with whom he sympathised profoundly, he seems to have been cured of the hallucinations of corpses in the London streets and the acute nervous strain that Graves observed. Life at Craiglockhart felt tedious, he was not free to come and go as he wished, there were very few people there who were congenial companions; his great diversion was to play golf and he was fortunate to find a course close to the grounds at Craiglockhart.

The irritation at not being allowed to sustain his protest continued through the summer of 1917. Distractions included visits from friends, including Robert Graves, and analysis of Wilfred Owen's growing dexterity in writing war poetry, but these were not enough to satisfy his uneasiness. Through conversations with Dr Rivers, Sassoon came to the decision that he could not alter the official management of the war or continue his protest effectively, but could only demonstrate his committed support for the men in the trenches by returning, leading them and caring for them as best he could. The sequence of events was not without its awkward moments, however – as when Sassoon, irritated at being kept waiting for the Medical Board that was to consider his case, stormed out of the building, causing great embarrassment to his admired Rivers.

The bonus from this period in hospital was Sassoon's own output of poems, a number of which were published in the *Hydra*, Craiglockhart's house journal. (The editor of the day was Wilfred Owen, directed to improve his mental state by exercising his enthusiasm for writing and passion for poetry. As well as his editorial contributions, the surviving copies of the *Hydra* from that summer show poems by Sassoon and Owen.) Sassoon's poems from this period demonstrate the full range of his sympathies and emotions; they include 'Does it Matter?', the fierce reflection on other people's casual kindness to the war-handicapped who can no longer join in their outdoor pastimes, or who are haunted by 'dreams from the pit'; a savage indictment of the complacent older generation in 'The Fathers'; and in 'Sick Leave' we can see his own feelings of guilt as he thinks of his active army life:

When I'm asleep, dreaming and lulled and warm, -
They come, the homeless ones, the noiseless dead.
While the dim charging breakers of the storm
Bellow and drone and rumble overhead,
Out of the gloom they gather about my bed.
They whisper to my heart; their thoughts are mine.
  'Why are you here with all your watches ended?
  From Ypres to Frise we sought you in the line'
In bitter safety I awake, unfriended;
And while the dawn begins with slashing rain

I think of the Battalion in the mud.
'When are you going out to them again?
Are they not still your brothers through our blood?'

Other poems hit out at the popular press, at Parliament, at women who admire heroes but ignore the uncomfortable truths about war – and, over and over again, devotion and sorrow, impotent anger at the terrible circumstances of the war and the tragedy of so many men whose future life is uselessly destroyed – 'Men who went out to battle, grim and glad;/Children, with eyes that hate you, broken and mad'. He grieves for his own losses too, for his inability to help 'the patient men who fight' ('Banishment').

There were other poems too, that looked back to more peaceful times and pre-war pastimes; 'Break of Day' was about hunting and was written for his old friend Gordon Harbord (ironically he began the poem, without knowing it, the day after Harbord was killed at Ypres).

GORDON HARBORD was killed in action on 14 August 1917, at the age of 27. A Lieutenant (Temporary Captain) with the Royal Field Artillery, he had won the Military Cross early in 1917. Gordon ('Stephen Colwood', in *Memoirs of a Fox-Hunting Man*) and his brother Geoffrey had been close friends of Sassoon's for several years, sharing a delight in hunting, cricket and facetious and quirky letters. His death came as a serious blow to Sassoon, who described him as 'my greatest friend before the war'. In one of his longer poems written at Craiglockhart, 'Break of Day', Sassoon brought together the miseries of war and the remembered delights of hunting days.

Captain Stephen Harbord, MC, Royal Field Artillery. His grave is in Vlamertinghe New Military Cemetery, near Ypres. In Sassoon's fictional memoirs, Harbord was 'Colwood', no doubt a reference to his parents' home address, Colwood Park.

Robert Graves did all that he could to protect and support Sassoon, although the intensity of their friendship was perhaps beginning to diminish. He too was in a seriously nervous state and, although he had several long talks with Rivers, he refused to undergo more extensive treatment with him out of fear of losing his creative drive. The summer of 1917 saw an improvement in his health, however, both physical and emotional – and his efforts to avoid a court martial being set up for Sassoon had considerably improved his standing in the Royal Welch Fusiliers. He spent August at Litherland Camp, instructing soldiers, enjoying sport – and further encouraged by the news that his collection of poems, *Fairies and Fusiliers*, was to be published in the autumn, with an American edition the next year. Although he later suppressed his war poems, they were reissued after his death and reveal his concern with the past and its relationship with the present. This covered many aspects of war, from references to Roman legions in ancient Gaul to the close companionship of 'Two Fusiliers' (himself and Sassoon) who were bound together by their shared experiences:

> *And have we done with War at last?*
> *Well, we've been lucky devils both,*
> *And there's no need of pledge or oath*
> *To bind our lovely friendship fast,*
> *By firmer stuff*
> *Close bound enough*
> *By wire and wood and stake we're bound,*
> *By Fricourt and by Festubert,*
> *By whipping rain, by the sun's glare,*
> *By all the misery and loud sound,*
> *By a Spring day,*
> *By Picard clay.*
> *Show me the two so closely bound*
> *As we by the wet bond of blood,*
> *By friendship blossoming from mud,*
> *By Death: we faced him, and we found*
> *Beauty in Death,*
> *In dead men, breath.*

The damp Mersey-side climate was bad for his damaged lungs, however, and late in September 1917 he was glad to be passed 'fit for garrison service' – Oswestry first, then Kinmel Camp near Rhyl, preparatory to a proposed posting to garrison duty in Egypt or Gibraltar. Leave before going overseas gave him the opportunity to spend time with Nancy Nicholson, an old friend who had come to hold an important place in his life and affections. Following a short-lived attraction to one of his nurses, Graves was relieved to find that he was now more interested in girls than in the boys or young men to whom he had hitherto been drawn.

No. 16 Officer Cadet Battn.

KINMEL PARK CAMP,
Nr. RHYL, N. WALES.

The Bearer of this Pass

Officer Cadet Docton H. L.

has leave of absence from Quarters.

R Graves Captain for

CMDG. "B" COY. No. 16. O. C. B.

Commanding............Company.

For time and date see last entry on inside of card. The
entry must bear initials of Company Commander.

Destination.	Time and Date From	To	Initials of O.C.Co.	Destination.	Time and Date From	To	Initials of O.C.Co.
Rhyl	2 PM 1 [?] 16	11-59 PM 1 [?] 16	Rf	Lancaster	7 AM 26/4/18	11-59 PM 3/5/18	RG
Theatre	6 pm March 23	11-59 PM March 23	Aart.		27/4/18	4/5/18	
St Asaph	10 AM 29/3/18	11 PM 29/3/18	Rf	Rhyl	6 PM 11/5/18	11-59 PM 11/5/18	RG
H Angele	2 PM 31/3/18	11 PM 31/3/18	Rf				
Colwyn Bay (by road)	10 AM 1/4/18 7 PM	11 PM 1/4/18 11 PM	Rf By road C.J.C.O				
Oswestri	6/4/18	6/4/18					
Rhyl	2 PM 20/4/18	6 P.M. 20/4/18	C.J.C.O				

No. 16 Officer Cadet Battalion. Leave Pass signed by Robert Graves and issued to Officer Cadet Docton when he was in training at Kinmel Park Camp, North Wales, March-May 1918. Entries giving permission to visit Rhyl, St Asaph and Abergele in March have been initialled by Graves acting on behalf of the Company Commander. {LEEMING}

KINMEL PARK CAMP

This training camp built in 1915 lies alongside the present-day A55 trunk route near the village of Bodelwyddan, between St.Asaph and Abergele. Six miles to the north is the town of Rhyl, on the main Crewe to Holyhead railway line with narrow-gauge railway access to the camp during the war. It was well located both for training and for despatching reinforcements, useful in preparing troops for active service in both World Wars. The camp consisted of more than twenty individual barrack complexes and a full complement of shops, canteens, churches and entertainment facilities. In 1917-18, in addition to several units involved in training young soldiers, two Officer Cadet training battalions, No. 16 and No. 17, which had senior instructors with considerable active service abroad. These two battalions were part of around a score which were formed in July 1917; this followed a decision that in future candidates for a commission would pass through an Officer Cadet Battalion, usually 400/600 strong, candidates would be at least 18 1/2 years old and would have served in the ranks. Graves was allocated to No.16 Officer Cadet battalion as one of its instructors.

Shortly after the end of hostilities (and after Graves's departure), Kinmel Camp gained some notoriety when members of the Canadian Army rioted in November 1918. No. 16 and No. 17 Officer Cadet battalions were called on to restore order. After a relative quiet period more unrest and disobedience followed, mainly concerned with the delay in returning the Canadians to their homeland, a situation not improved by the immediate repatriation of men who had never seen active service in preference to those who had.

Early in March 1919 the whole position deteriorated seriously, with looting of shops, canteens, Officers' and Sergeants' Messes and attacks by Canadians on Guard Rooms to release their comrades held in detention. Rioters were seen carrying red flags, adding a political slant to the riots which even the arrival of cavalry failed to control. Later, shots were exchanged and when the riots were finally quelled on the evening of 5 March, it was discovered that five Canadian soldiers had been killed and some twenty wounded. The dead soldiers were buried in the grounds of the distinctive marble church at Bodelwyddan on 8 March 1919 where, apart from the body of one serviceman whose remains were removed to Canada, they rest today.

On 12 October 1917 Graves took the night train to Edinburgh to visit

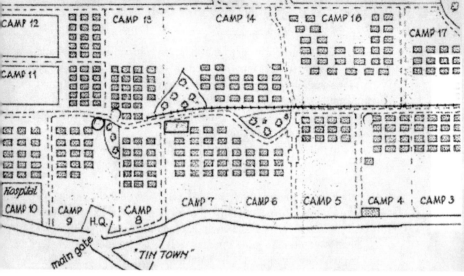

Sketch map of Kinmel Park Camp. In 1917-18 Robert Graves served here as an instructor to one of the Officer Cadet training battalions, leaving just before the Canadian Army disturbances in November 1918.

Sassoon once more, and met Wilfred Owen during the visit. He shared Sassoon's opinion of Owen's talent and gave him various bits of technical advice to advance his writing, reinforcing Sassoon's enthusiastic urging to 'sweat your guts out writing poetry'. Owen deeply appreciated the two men's help, and was delighted to be invited to Graves's marriage, in January 1918.

Early in November Graves's posting to Egypt was postponed; the fit men of the Third Garrison Battalion at Kinmel Park were ordered to Cork while Graves remained in command of eighty officers and 600 men.

Two weeks after Graves's visit, Sassoon was summoned before a

Kinmel Park Camp YMCA Theatre. The theatre buildings lay close to the main St. Asaph-Abergele road, and escaped damage during the various disturbances in 1918-19. However, the YMCA canteens, one of which lay along the road on the left of the photograph, were looted.

Medical Board. Earlier in the year, Graves and others had made tremendous efforts to steer him into medical care rather than a military prison; now, similar efforts were made to ensure that he was returned to active duty – for Sassoon had stated clearly that he would not return to duty unless he was guaranteed an immediate return to the Front. Although he was not in a position to dictate terms, it suited everyone concerned to fall in with this proposal; on 26 November he was passed for General Service and, as he commented, was once more 'an officer and a gentleman'.

He left Edinburgh for Litherland the same day and then went on leave, returning on 11 December 1917 to await orders. Golf at Formby Golf Club, where officers at the camp had honorary membership, was an excellent way of passing the time, as well as taking long walks and dining expensively at the Adelphi hotel in Liverpool. On Christmas day, after more golf, he had dinner with the Camp's Commanding Officer, Lieutenant-Colonel Jones-Williams at his house in nearby Crosby.

Captain J. V. Higginson, MC, 2nd Royal Welch Fusiliers. Died 23 September 1918, buried in Knockin, Shropshire. Captain Higginson was wounded twice, in June 1915 and again in July 1916; his death was attributed not only to the wounds but also to inhalation of gas in the closing months of the war.

Early in January 1918, he was transferred to New Barracks, Limerick, to join the recently-arrived 3rd Royal Welch. Litherland had been pleasant enough, but he was delighted to join comrades in Limerick and meet some of his comrades with whom he had served in the past and who, like Sassoon, were awaiting drafting overseas. Among the 120 officers in the barracks was Captain J. V. Higginson who had been with Sassoon when they were both sent to join the 1st Royal Welch at Festubert in November 1915.

Sassoon continued with his poetry, which seems to express sad weariness rather than the fierce irony of the time at Craiglockhart: poems from the Limerick period include 'Invocation', 'Memory', 'Remorse' and 'Dead Musicians'. 'Together' relates the mood at the end of a day's fox-hunting haunted by a companionable ghostly figure – a memory of Gordon Harbord.

144

Sassoon could have been sent as a reinforcement to the 2nd Royal Welch in the Ypres Salient who were about to join the 38th (Welsh) Division or to his favourite battalion, the 1st Royal Welch, now in Italy; but to his disappointment the orders that came through on 21 January 1918 sent him to join the 25th (Montgomeryshire & Welsh Horse) Battalion Royal Welch Fusiliers presently serving with the 231st Brigade of the 74th (Yeomanry) Division in Palestine, as part of the Egyptian Expeditionary Force. The Division had been in existence for some twelve months, made up of eighteen dismounted Yeomanry regiments, the majority of which, like the Welsh Horse and Sassoon's former regiment, the Sussex Yeomanry, had fought in Gallipoli.

2nd ROYAL WELCH AND 38th (WELSH) DIVISION

By January 1918, the number of 'Old Army' men in the Battalion was negligible. In 1914 most of the battalion, often known as the Birmingham Fusiliers, came from England and were heavy beer drinkers. The composition had now changed with a majority of men coming from North Wales whose habits of social recreation were different; to the surprise of the Battalion's officers, up to 40% of the men asked for coffee rather than beer. In the Transport, Corps of Drums and Signals section, however, the home of the surviving Old Army men, coffee drinkers were unknown and beer drinking continued as the popular pastime.

Sassoon travelled via Dublin and London to report in Southampton by Monday 11 February. The Irish Sea was dangerous at the time, from the activities of the German submarine U.101 which had sunk the S.S. *Mexico City* with heavy loss of life a few days earlier, but he encountered no problems and continued onwards to reach Cherbourg well before dawn on 12 February. Here he was in a rest camp with a group of officers that included Lieutenant S.W. Harper who, with Robert Graves, had been part of the military escort deputed to accompany Sassoon to Craiglockhart in July 1917. (They missed the rendezvous and Sassoon travelled alone to Edinburgh.) Two days later he set off on an enjoyable train journey of almost 1500 miles through France and Italy, reaching Taranto on 21 February 1918.

The transit camp in Taranto accommodated officers of many different units, ranging in rank from staff-officers and colonels to more lowly subalterns, including officers of the 38th Royal Fusiliers, one of three recently formed Fusilier battalions composed entirely of Jewish

SS *Kashgar*. The P&O liner in which Sassoon sailed from Italy to Egypt in February 1918.

General Headquarters, Egyptian Expeditionary Force, Cairo. A photograph taken outside the barbed wire perimeter of General Allenby's Headquarters. The soldier, employed as a stenographer on the General's staff, is wearing the uniform of a sapper in the Signals Section of the Royal Engineers. Note the helmet, riding breeches and spurs. Allenby was later to give orders that riding breeches and spurs were not to be worn without reason whilst on active service in Palestine; looser and more practical uniform clothing was to be worn instead. <small>COPYRIGHT P.W. GUEST.</small>

volunteers. Like Sassoon it had recently reached Taranto from England on its way to Alexandria, before moving on to Palestine to see service under General Allenby.

After a break of three days he boarded the S.S. *Kashgar* to cross the Mediterranean and three days later reached the Egyptian port of Alexandria, in a region which in 1914 was nominally part of the Ottoman Empire: in 1915 the Turkish Army made repeated attempts to breach the British Line, particularly at the floating bridge at El Kantara on the Suez Canal, but fortunately it had been held and the vital canal remained safely in British hands.

By 2 March 1918 Sassoon was at the dreary British No.1 Base Depot at El Kantara. Here, as in the previous year near Arras, he was once again under the overall command of General Allenby, now Commander-in-Chief, Egyptian Expeditionary Force and whose victorious army had recently captured Jerusalem and Jericho.

146

Allenby had not had a particularly successful campaign whilst commanding Third Army at the Battle of Arras and his recall to London for interview in June 1917 seemed likely to be the prelude to his removal from the appointment. To his surprise, however, he was offered the Palestine Command as replacement for the ill-fated Sir Archibald Murray, whose leadership had sometimes been seen to be less than positive. On his arrival in Cairo later the same month, the newly confident Allenby (who was known as 'The Bull') began to rehabilitate his new command – although he suffered a devastating blow a month later with the news that his only child, Lieutenant Michael Allenby, had died of wounds in Belgium.

His successes in taking Damascus and Aleppo by October 1918 (despite the departures of the 52nd (Lowland) and 74th (Yeomanry) Divisions to France in April 1918) proved the wisdom of his appointment. One of Allenby's far-reaching decisions to bear fruit was to have confidence in the remarkable T.E. Lawrence, who was eventually to become a close friend of Graves. In 1927 Graves sought Allenby's opinion of the widespread 'Lawrence of Arabia' legend before the publication of his book *Lawrence and the Arabs*. Sassoon and Lawrence also became firm friends, and Lawrence was one of the guests at Sassoon's marriage in 1933.

General Sir Edmund H. H. Allenby. Sassoon, serving with the 2nd RWF, briefly came under the General's command in 1917 during the Arras battles and again in 1918 with 25th Royal Welch Fusiliers in Palestine when Allenby was Commander in Chief of the Egyptian Expeditionary Force.

Part of Allenby's success, however, must be attributed to his predecessor's insistence on the construction of a pipe-line to supply the front line with water from the River Nile, some 120 miles away, and a military railway to carry troops and supplies into Palestine. It was on this railway that Sassoon, travelling in a cattle-truck, crossed the Sinai peninsula. He reached Gaza on the morning of 10 March 1918 and continued to Ludd, at the end of the railway line. He arrived in the afternoon of 11 March, still some twenty miles from his Battalion.

The tented rest-camp set up about a mile from Ludd railway station was not to Sassoon's liking. No doubt, however, it was preferable to the severe fighting in which the 25th Royal Welch were engaged that day, in an attack at Sinjil some ten miles north-west of Jericho. There were several officer casualties in the attack, which proved to be the last

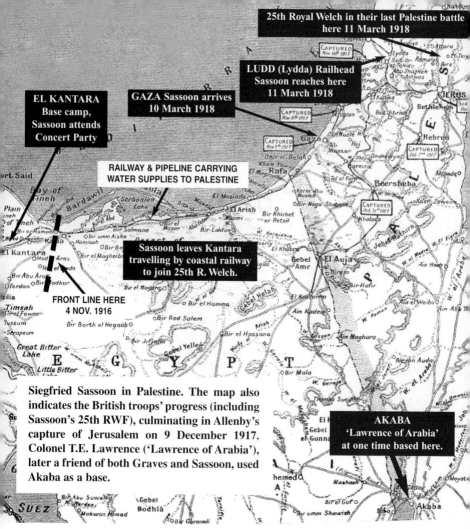

25th Royal Welch in their last Palestine battle here 11 March 1918

LUDD (Lydda) Railhead Sassoon reaches here 11 March 1918

GAZA Sassoon arrives 10 March 1918

EL KANTARA Base camp, Sassoon attends Concert Party

RAILWAY & PIPELINE CARRYING WATER SUPPLIES TO PALESTINE

Sassoon leaves Kantara travelling by coastal railway to join 25th R. Welch.

FRONT LINE HERE 4 NOV. 1916

Siegfried Sassoon in Palestine. The map also indicates the British troops' progress (including Sassoon's 25th RWF), culminating in Allenby's capture of Jerusalem on 9 December 1917. Colonel T.E. Lawrence ('Lawrence of Arabia'), later a friend of both Graves and Sassoon, used Akaba as a base.

AKABA 'Lawrence of Arabia' at one time based here.

required of the Battalion in Palestine.

Thirty-four days after leaving Ireland, Sassoon finally reported to the 25th Royal Welch on 14 March, travelling via Jerusalem and Rahm Alla where he met Sergeant L. Stone of the 16th Royal Sussex (formerly the Sussex Yeomanry) with whom he had served in 1914. (Later promoted to Company Sergeant Major, Stone was wounded on 21 September 1918 in France and taken prisoner during the final advance to victory on a day when Battalion casualties numbered 355.)

The 25th Royal Welch, which Sassoon joined in March 1918, had shifted from its Yeomanry role to that of a Welsh infantry battalion within the previous 12 months. The intention for the new unit which was raised in Cardiff on 2 August 1914 was that it would be a Welsh

Cavalry Regiment, and for this reason it was named the 1st/1st The Welsh Horse. Recruits flocked to join it from all over South Wales. The commanding officer was a seasoned soldier and colourful veteran of the South African War – Captain A. O. Vaughan who had Hugh Edwardes, the 6th Lord Kensington, late 15th Hussars and a well known Pembrokeshire land owner, as his Adjutant. Despite expectations of existence as a Welsh Cavalry Regiment, it was established as a Territorial Force Yeomanry Regiment under the Glamorgan Territorial Association, presided over by the Earl of Plymouth. Unfortunately for Captain Vaughan, he was looked down on locally and, with the warm approval of the War Office, his devoted assistant Lord Kensington was appointed in command of the regiment. Vaughan was promoted to the rank of major, and transferred to the 14th Northumberland Fusiliers. He ended the war as a lieutenant-colonel, winning the Distinguished Service Order.

There was disappointment in South Wales when The Welsh Horse's Regimental Depot, widely expected to be in Cardiff from where so many recruits had enlisted, was established in Newtown, Montgomeryshire – an area with little if any connection with the regiment. With their training completed, The Welsh Horse (without horses) reached Gallipoli by 8 October 1915; here it was mistakenly assumed that a regiment from South Wales would include a substantial

Officers of the Welsh Horse Yeomanry. The Yeomanry later became the 25th (Montgomeryshire and Welsh Horse Yeomanry) Battalion Royal Welsh Fusiliers, which Sassoon joined in Palestine in 1918. Lieutenant-Colonel Lord Kensington, to whom Sassoon took a dislike but who served with distinction as Commanding Officer for most of its war service, is seated in the centre of the front row. TRUSTEES OF THE WELCH REGIMENT MUSEUM.

number of ex-miners in their ranks – resulting in its quite unsuitable conversion into a Pioneer battalion. After the evacuation of the Gallipoli Peninsula, The Welsh Horse was sent to Egypt where it again continued as a dismounted unit. Eventually, in March 1917 and now part of the newly formed 74th Division, it combined with the 1st/1st Montgomeryshire Yeomanry to form an infantry battalion in the Royal Welch Fusiliers with Lord Kensington in command.

'A VERY BAD TYPE OF BRITISH NOBLEMAN'

Sassoon's diary for 5 April 1918 records a disdainful opinion of his Colonel, Lord Kensington, describing him as 'both vulgar and snobbish' and declaring that he would look very much at home in the cheaper public enclosures at a race-meeting. This scathing condemnation of Kensingon seems excessive, for the colonel had commanded the Brigade Rearguard during the Gallipoli evacuation and came to Egypt under the demanding command of General Allenby. The immediate cause of Sassoon's distaste was an Officers' Mess 'sweep', set up by Lord Kensington, on the Battalion's ultimate destination. Fulminating against the ridiculous prices offered for tickets, Sassoon eventually, and with bad grace, bid £10 for a ticket entitled 'Submarined'.

Kensington was eventually on active service in command of The Welsh Horse until in August 1918 he handed the battalion over to Lieutenant-Colonel Rees, DSO, for the remaining three months of the war.

A period of relaxation for the battalion followed at a rest camp at Nablus where Sassoon shared a tent with Captain F.R. Charlesworth, an Oxford graduate, and where he seems to have spent a lot of his time walking the countryside enjoying the peaceful atmosphere. (Charlesworth was to die of wounds received during the Battle of Epehy in September 1918, a battle in which Sergeant Waring of the 25th Royal Welch won his V.C.). Soon this was to change. News reached the camp of the German breakthrough in France on 21 March 1918 and by 7 April the battalion was on the move from Palestine, beginning a long route march to the railway terminus at Ludd and passing General Allenby along the way.

The German Army had begun a series of offensives on the Western Front, beginning on 21 March 1918 and finally ending on 17 July. The Allied Armies were pushed back over many miles, the position was desperate and an Allied defeat was not impossible. However, as reverse

Palestine. Tents of a Royal Army Service Corps base, with camels in the background belonging to one of the RASC transport companies of General Allenby's Egyptian Expeditionary Force. Some 40,000 camels were eventually employed, and were particularly useful in bringing up supplies when a water shortage prevented the use of horses in desert conditions. By 1918 the Camel Transport Corps had engaged some 20,000 Egyptian drivers on six-monthly contracts.

An Egyptian Driver.

followed reverse reinforcements were suddenly made available and in a period of some five months well over half a million men were despatched from the regimental depots in the U.K. to help stem the German onslaught. Still more men were needed, Italy was combed for reinforcements and two British divisions and several battalions were found and sent to France. Twelve battalions were recalled from Salonika and it was now that Allenby was instructed to release the 52nd (Lowland) Division and the 74th (Yeomanry) Division (including the 25th Royal Welch) with immediate effect. As and when they could be spared another 23 battalions were withdrawn from the Egyptian Expeditionary Force and sent to the Western Front, providing a grand total from these overseas battlefields of over 100,000 men. In the end the numbers were sufficient and on 8 August 1918 the tide turned in the Allies' favour.

By this time the American Expeditionary Force (A.E.F.) was beginning to take an important share in the Allies' advance to victory, battles which were in progress along the Western Front from the English Channel to Verdun and beyond. In September 1918 the First American Army consisted of twenty combat divisions. However, some seven U.S. Army divisions were left with the British and French armies, the 27th and 30th divisions in particular being allocated to General Rawlinson's Fourth Army.

From August 1918 until the Armistice there was seldom a day in

A US Army infantryman, 1918.

which American soldiers were not engaged in action, either alongside the British and French armies or down in the valley of the Meuse with their own First American Army. Between October 1917 and the Armistice in November 1918 the ultimate victory cost the A.E.F. losses of over 260,000 battle casualties, of whom 50,000 were killed – an indication of the U.S. effort during the Great War.

Starting out on 11 April, the 25th Royal Welch set out from Ludd to Egypt in a long train of cattle trucks. (This was the date of Field Marshal Haig's famous 'Backs to the Wall' Order of the Day to all the British Forces in France, designed to counter a situation seen as critical.) The battalion reached El Kantara the following morning and Sassoon was now back at the despised Base Camp he had left some six weeks before. Amidst the battalion training and reorganisation, however, the camp was not without entertainment, for Sassoon joined the troops to attend a show given by the Lena Ashwell Concert Party.

THE CONCERT PARTY

Lena Ashwell was an accomplished actress and impresario who arranged concerts to entertain troops on rest behind the front lines. Always well attended, the concerts were staged in France as well as in the Middle East and her contribution to forces' morale during the war earned her the OBE. She died in 1957.

The performance at Kantara inspired Sassoon's poem 'Concert Party (Egyptian Base Camp)', a quiet and atmospheric evocation of nostalgia and homesickness rather than brash or raucous choruses, and in his diary entry about it he reflects on the soldiers' longing for 'LIFE with its song and dance – life with its brief gaiety'. He recognises the intensity of feeling in the audience, gazing at puppet-like performers, and is aware of the ghosts of the war-dead.

152

Lena Ashwell's Concert Party. Sassoon records his attendance at a performance by this concert party in 1918, in camp in Egypt.

> While the poem ends in sad resignation, the diary entry shows his feelings of doom and his desperation to get away from this entertainment in the sand. Two days later his diary refers to it as 'very impressive', commenting that the scene moved him more than anything since he left England.

Orders were soon received for the Division to leave Egypt for the Western Front, where it was urgently needed. Sassoon remarked that some of the men had been overseas for over two years; they were now pleased to be travelling over two thousand miles to the bloody battlefields of France since it seemed nearer home than the Egyptian desert. Wounded men from the Divisional units in Cairo, hearing that the Battalion was destined to leave Egypt, immediately sought their discharge from hospital – some joined the Battalion without even an official discharge and clearly not fully recovered from their wounds.

The Battalion left Gabbari Docks, Alexandria, on 1 May 1918 on board RMS *Malwa*, accompanied by H.M.Transport *Caledonia* (which was carrying men of the former Sussex Yeomanry with whom Sassoon had served in 1914) and the Union Castle Liner *Leasowe Castle*, part of a convoy of seven fast merchantmen on passage for Marseilles in the south of France. For the past few weeks these ships had been employed solely in transporting troops from the Middle East to France. The *Malwa* was a former P&O liner of some 11,000 tons, operating in peace time on the India and China Passenger and Mail service and carrying 600 passengers, but accommodating more than three thousand men as a troopship.

Sassoon's diary entry reflects a sense of isolation from his fellow-

Suez Canal. These British and Indian soldiers have just crossed by barge from the Egyptian side of the canal to an encampment being established on its opposite bank.

officers. The sea voyage was a relaxing interval which gave him leisure to observe and comment, and his notes record his interpretations. What he calls the 'mental deadness' around him, a refusal to face facts, was perceived as an effective form of protection against the battlefield that awaited them; the favoured past-times for his fellow-officers revolved around bridge, army gossip and drink. He watched the Other Ranks, relaxing and lying indolently on the sunlit deck, with much greater pleasure, enjoying the sight of their warm companionship; his description for their affection for each other, and his own self-awareness, was 'pathetic and beautiful and human (but that is only a sexual emotion in me to like them in those attitudes)'. He described himself as 'confused ... intolerant and superficial' together with a desire to plunge back into the terrors of the war – yet without believing that he would really kill people or 'help in the destruction of human life ... But I am throwing off my haunting fears and apprehensions. *No limelight, please!*' This long and revealing diary entry ends with some

Suez Canal. A British Army outpost on the banks of the Suez Canal in 1918.

self-mockery at his own 'mental hotch-potch'.

Sassoon also later recorded the journey in his poem 'Night on the Convoy (Alexandria – Marseilles)', an atmospheric description with long lines that echo the steady movement of the ship. In it, he refers to the sleeping soldiers on the deck and recalls similar men dead at Arras.

AFLOAT IN THE MEDITERRANEAN
IN THE FIRST WORLD WAR

Allied shipping of every type, troopships, transports carrying mail, cattle ships loaded with mules, and even hospital ships were fruitful prey for Austrian-Hungarian and German submarines as they criss-crossed the Mediterranean. In 1917, for example, the German submarine UC 74 (Lieutenant-Commander W. Marschall) sank the Royal Mail Steam Packet Company liner *Arcadian* with 1,000 troops on board, of whom almost a quarter (including eight doctors and thirty orderlies from the RAMC, and 35 of the crew) went down with the ship. A convoy system introduced in October of that year reduced the number of sinkings but the escorts frequently lacked expertise and losses continued. Vessels were not even immune from attack at the entrance to Alexandria harbour, for at the end of December 1917, and within 24 hours of each other, the *Aragon* and the *Osmanieh* fell victim to the German submarine UC34.

Austrian submarines were no less active, although a mutiny in the Austrian Navy in February 1918 helped to reduce losses. (One successful U-boat commander was Lieutenant G. von Trapp who later won a different kind of fame in a different war, with his singing family and the well-known film *The Sound of Music*). In March, Leutnant Karl Dönitz (later Grand Admiral Dönitz of Hitler's Navy) was in action torpedoing shipping and later received a decoration on the Kaiser's personal instructions; eventually his submarine was sunk and he became a Prisoner of War of the British.

Stories were circulating in May, as Sassoon's convoy made its way to a safe landfall off Marseilles, that the ships had been threatened by numerous German and Austrian submarines as they steamed through the Mediterranean. In fact the British naval position had improved, for in May the German U-boat fleet in the Mediterranean suffered its heaviest losses so far, four of them being sunk in that month. Sassoon noted, however, that the Union Castle liner *Leasowe Castle*, just two years old and serving as a troopship, was sunk in the subsequent Alexandria to Marseilles convoy by the German submarine UB51 on 27 May, some 104 miles from its Egyptian port of departure. The heavy losses of those on board came to 92, including the Master, 46 Officers and men of the Nottinghamshire Yeomanry (South Notts Hussars), 21 from the Machine Gun Corps and 9 from the Warwickshire Yeomanry.

Sassoon's luck held true, for the *Malwa* reached port unscathed, although six ships were sunk out of ten of her class. Steady seamanship saved the *Malwa* on one occasion – a rapid alteration of course meant that a German torpedo running towards the ship struck only a glancing blow on the hull, and an explosion was avoided. On a later voyage in the Irish Sea she rammed and sank a German U-boat, one of only six merchant ships to destroy a submarine during the war. She resumed a Far East service in 1920 and was broken up twelve years later.

On 7 May 1918 the Battalion moved into No 10 Rest Camp just outside Marseilles, and that evening Sassoon and two other officers were invited to dine with Lord Kensington. Later they went on to a Music Hall; the pleasant evening and conversation seemed to give Sassoon a more favourable opinion of his commanding officer. By 13 May the unit had reached Domvast, some eight miles from Abbeville.

SS *Leasowe Castle*. A twin-screw coal burning steamer built by Cammell Laird of Birkenhead. Taken over in 1917 by the British Government (from the Greek government), it was operated as a troopship by the Union Castle Line. It was torpedoed by U35 under the command of Kapitänleutnant de la Perière (who became the highest scoring submarine captain of the war, with a total of nearly 200 Allied ships sunk), it reached Gibraltar for repairs and was finally sunk by UB 51 on 27 May 1918. Note the camouflage design on the hull. R.MELLOR.

RMS *Malwa*. The steamship in which Sassoon and his battalion, the 25th RWF, took passage from Alexandria to Marseilles in May 1918.

Chapter Eight

BACK TO THE WESTERN FRONT

Although the Battalion had seen much fighting in both Gallipoli and Palestine, the men now needed re-equipping, instruction and training for poison gas (a weapon that was useless in Palestine) and also practice in working with tanks. Sassoon, involved in much of this work, was also required to take care of his company's comfort - a task to which he had never before given so much time and energy. Some of the training was carried out around 35 miles from the fighting, in the Forest of Crécy - the site, as Sassoon noted, of the Battle of Crécy 572 years earlier. The Division was introduced to the new but well-received experience of billeting, with some men lodged in barns and others in houses in the nearby village of Domvast. A figure from Sassoon's past reappeared, Major Campbell with his famous blood-curdling exposition of bayonet fighting; Sassoon had disliked the lecture at the Fourth Army School at Flixécourt in 1916, but now it apparently went down well with his men.

There was a break from training when the whole Brigade marched to the village of Cauchy, on the Abbeville road. Here, with the men formed into a hollow square, Major-General Girdwood awarded the Victoria Cross to a young soldier from Oswestry - Harold Whitfield of the 10th King's Shropshire Light Infantry. He had won the decoration in Palestine and his Battalion was now serving alongside the 25th Royal Welch in the same brigade. Sassoon's men were not impressed by the General's glowing remarks as he presented the medal (it was the K.S.L.I.'s only V.C. of the Great War), as they had been given insufficient time to finish their meal before marching off to witness the ceremony. Sassoon thought the whole show absurd and, perhaps unfairly, described it as simply a morale-boosting exercise.

By 25 May 1918 the Battalion had moved forward to the crowded village of Habarcq some twelve miles to the west of Arras. The Battalion officers found comfortable quarters in the château, with Sassoon in a large room on an upper storey. With the absence of one of the officers on leave he became acting Company Commander of A

Private Harold Whitfield, VC, 10th Kings Shropshire Light Infantry. Siegfried Sassoon was on the parade when Whitfield was presented with his medal, awarded for gallantry on 10 March 1918 during enemy counter attacks on the battalion's position at Burj El Lisaneh, Egypt

157

Company for the following five weeks, which required him to supervise further training and to attend various conferences from time to time. It also involved him in a brief attachment to a Canadian battalion, the 24th Battalion CEF (Victoria Rifles) in the line at Neuville-Vitasse, south of Arras, a form of refresher in warfare for Sassoon.

The training and rest came to an end. On 20 June the 74th Division was on the move, the 25th Royal Welch battalion leaving Habarcq for St. Hilaire, 15 miles west of Béthune. A strange illness was invading the Division, however: a worrying number of cases were recorded in May of what was known as 'three-day fever', an illness of unknown origin. By the time the battalions moved forward the impact of the illness was increasing, and the number of cases in June and July was to cause serious concern. (This seems to have been an outbreak of Spanish 'flu, part of the pandemic that would ultimately take more lives than the First World War itself.)

When the 25th Royal Welch left Palestine en route for France they were part of the response to an urgent need for men to repel the German offensive, in which a breakthrough to the Channel ports was not wholly impossible. The strategic position had changed for the better since their arrival in France and the whole Division learned that trench warfare was not now envisaged: they were to be part of a nucleus being formed to bring victory in 1919! In the event, the Battalion eventually took its place in the front line in the River Lys sector, where a strong German attack had driven back the Allied front line.

Any thought of victory would have been laughable just a few weeks previously, when there was a serious danger of an Allied defeat; on 9 April 1918 the enemy struck decisively along a front extending seventeen miles north from the La Bassée canal where the 55th (West Lancashire) Division held the line. One of the brigades of that Division holding the front near Festubert was commanded by Brigadier-General Stockwell - formerly of the 1st Royal Welch, under whom Sassoon and Graves had served at the Bois Français trenches in 1916. It was to stand fast and serve the Allied cause well. On its left, however, three brigades of the Portuguese Army maintained a thinly-held front line of waterlogged trenches facing four strong German divisions.

It was a recipe for disaster. The Portuguese soldiers had no interest in the conduct of the war, for their Government was participating purely for political reasons and the troops' resistance proved minimal. By 4.30 am on 9 April the weak Portuguese division was quickly

Troops of the Portuguese army on the march. When the German Army went on the offensive again in April 1918, the front line around Laventie was held by three weak Portuguese brigades. They were quickly overwhelmed by four German divisions, and forced to retire in some disorder. British troops stabilised the front line around Saint Floris, where Sassoon arrived some weeks later with the 25th RWF.

overwhelmed by the German attack, cut off and driven back. Very fierce fighting followed as British reserves moved into action, but it was not until 17 April that they were able to stabilise the front in the sector between the River Lys and Robecq village, a distance of about 4000 yards in which men of the 61st (2nd/South Midland) Division played a prominent part. So great was the threat of a breakthrough here that as units of this division de-trained they were immediately loaded into buses and sent into combat piecemeal, as soon as they arrived. It was in this area that the 25th Royal Welch now moved into the front

Les Amusoires. A recent view of a farm in the hamlet of Les Amusoires, possibly used as Battalion Headquarters during the period when Sassoon's Royal Welch were occupying the front line nearby. Note the concrete bunker of 1918 vintage to the right of the picture.

BUNKER

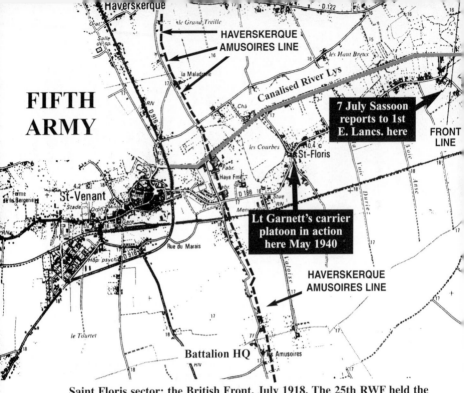

Saint Floris sector; the British Front, July 1918. The 25th RWF held the line here in July 1918, where the Haverskerque-Amusoires line was regarded as the last line of defence, to be held at all costs. Sassoon was wounded on 13 July, whilst on patrol beyond the front line. Part of the British 'advance to victory' began from this front, on 8 August 1918.

line.

The sector's front line consisted of a series of breastworks usually described as 'grouse butts', each occupied by a platoon, for the high water table here meant that conventional trenches would quickly become waterlogged. For this reason the posts were joined, if at all, by a line of shallow depressions scooped out of the ground - a system well-known to Sassoon from his days in the Festubert area in 1915. The barbed wire entanglements were often hidden in standing corn and very basic, but the men who held these positions were none the less expected to delay an advancing enemy until reinforcements could be brought up to mount a counter-attack. Back in the support line the grouse butts were more numerous and closer together. Much farther back still lay the last line of defence - another series of strong-points stretching north of Robecq, from Les Amusoires across the canalised River Lys to Haverskerque and known to the troops as the 'amusing haversack line'. Les Amusoires Farm, which possessed a deep cellar, was generally used for the battalions' headquarters.

During daylight it was almost impossible to move between the grouse butts without drawing sniper fire but even so the area was known to be a quiet one. At night it was difficult to supply the outlying posts along tracks cut through the ripening corn, which had grown to a considerable height. This was the area that the 74th Division was to take over, and on 7 July Sassoon received instructions to contact the 1st East Lancashires in the front line of the St.Floris sector, and to make arrangements for the 25th Royal Welch to take over. (The 1st East Lancashires, a regular battalion, had only recently been transferred to the 61st Division, where they had received a draft of 300 experienced soldiers, and had been in the line since 9 June.)

The church at St Floris. Badly damaged during the fighting in 1918. The road junction in front of the church was also the scene of fighting on 23 May 1940, when Lieutenant John B Garnett, son of Lieutenant-Colonel W.B. Garnett (Sassoon's former Commanding Officer), was killed in an action involving a German anti-tank gun. Later, the gun was destroyed by a Bren-gun carrier crew at a nearby fork in the road, just behind the camera position.

SAINT FLORIS SECTOR

In 1918 the church in this small village was very badly damaged by shell-fire and because of its proximity to the front line was known as Hell Fire Corner. It was well known to Sassoon and his men of the Royal Welch Fusiliers as they passed it on their way to the nearby front line. In May 1940 it was again well known to the Regiment, for the Bren-Gun carrier Platoon of the 1st Battalion was in action against a German anti-tank gun guarding the cross roads by the church during the British retreat to Dunkirk. One officer, a sergeant and five men, some of them involved in the action, are buried by the church: the officer is Lieutenant John Brooksbank Garnett, the 23-year-old son of Lieutenant-Colonel W. B. Garnett DSO, DL, JP - who had been Sassoon's Commanding Officer when Sassoon was serving in the 2nd Battalion in April 1917, on the Arras front. (Lieutenant-Colonel Garnett was the officer who was admonished by the Corps Commander taking the salute by the roadside as the battalion marched by on its way to Arras, for his failure to dismount when reporting to his superior officer.)

During the fighting on 23 May 1940 Colonel Garnett's son commanding the leading carrier, and his men had forced the Germans with their anti-tank gun by the side of the church to withdraw. Unfortunately as the two carriers, the second commanded by Sergeant Spilsted, reached the fork in the road just to the west of the village they were both destroyed by German anti-tank guns in position further along the road towards Saint Venant. Corporal Jones and his men in the third carrier moved forward and they in turn destroyed the guns which had killed their comrades. Lieutenant Garnett and his Sergeant lie alongside each other in graves 5 and 6 by the side of St. Floris church. In 1951 the Commonwealth War Graves Commission appealed to the Royal Welch Fusiliers for help in a positive identification of the graves of Lieutenant Garnett and two of his men. With the help of the Regimental Old Comrades Association, a former corporal in Garnett's Carrier platoon - R. E. Jarvis - later came forward with the required information; the Commission was able to put up headstones over Lieutenant Garnett's grave and those of his crew - Fusiliers Clegg and Davies.

The British connection with Saint Floris in the Great War is commemorated by cement reproductions of the cap badges of

Saint Floris Memorials. The scene of much fighting in 1918. The church, known as 'Hell Fire Corner', was just behind the lines on 7 July when Sassoon moved to the sector. To the left of the village war memorial, a brick wall commemorates the battalions of the 61st and 74th Divisions who fought here in 1918, with reproductions of their cap badges. In May 1940 the Bren Gun Carrier Platoon of the 1st RWF, advancing along the road from the right of the photograph, came under fire from a German anti-tank gun nearby. Some of the crews who were killed lie in the row of graves on the right.

Saint Floris Church. Two of the regimental cap badges on the commemorative wall. Both seen here have a connection with Sassoon: on the left, the badge of the 25th RWF, with whom Sassoon served in 1918 in the British front line near here, and on the right, the badge of the 16th Royal Sussex, formerly the Sussex Yeomanry, in which Sassoon enlisted in 1914.

> those regiments of the 61st and 74th Divisions which occupied the village in 1918 set in a brick wall beside the French War memorial, and the graves of the Royal Welch killed in 1940.

It was a confident and efficient Sassoon who reported to the East Lancashires for details of the changeover arrangements. (No doubt the fact that he represented a former dismounted Yeomanry regiment was offset, in the eyes of officers of this regular battalion, by the ribbon of the Military Cross on his tunic.) Company Headquarters was near the front line, in a shell-hole where Sassoon was warmly welcomed by some East Lancashires officers, one of them preoccupied with arrangements for an imminent raid on the German trenches designed to capture a prisoner for identification purposes. The attacking party was formed of two platoons, consisting of two officers and fifty other ranks. It was not a success: no prisoner was taken, Second Lieutenants Innes and Morris were wounded and three men, one a sergeant, were killed. (These three are buried in St.Venant-Robecq Communal Cemetery). After continuing with trench familiarisation, Sassoon returned to his company a few hours later that evening, leading them to the front line.

Having witnessed the failed efforts of the East Lancashires' raiding party, Sassoon was determined to do a better job and at the same time to prove that Sassoon's A Company was militarily superior to the other companies in the Battalion. Perhaps he was inspired by his time with the two regular battalions of the Royal Welch and their practice of maintaining supremacy over No Man's Land. Very soon he was leading a patrol out towards the enemy lines, accompanied by Lieutenant Jowett and two NCOs to acclimatise them to the different conditions on the Western Front.

Sassoon's leadership was clearly commendable, but both officer-led patrols for indoctrination purposes and raids against the enemy were usually the task of second lieutenants and certainly not customary for experienced company commanders. Sassoon, who did not agree with this principle, laid on regular twenty-minute forays towards the German lines, taking pairs of soldiers with him on each of what he liked to describe as 'conducted tours'.

Sassoon's excursions into No Man's Land directly contradicted Brigade's orders that company commanders were not to go beyond the British barbed wire - yet he ignored these instructions, giving as a reason his need to get away from the irksome duties of company commander. One afternoon, for example, making a lone reconnaissance across to the German trenches with only a soldier's bayonet as a weapon, he entered one of the trenches and collected some German stick grenades on the way. Not surprisingly, he came across four soldiers manning a machine-gun post who, fortunately for him, disappeared into the surrounding corn as he returned rapidly to his own lines - to the relief of his friend and second-in-command, Lieutenant Vivian de Sola Pinto.

VIVIAN DE SOLA PINTO

In *Sherston's Progress*, Sassoon describes his pleasure and relief at finding himself supported by 'Velmore' - 'It was like having an extra head and a duplicate pair of eyes'. Vivian de Sola Pinto, who had interrupted his university career to enlist in the army, was to become a professor of English Literature, and was already a poet. He and Sassoon took great pleasure in discussing poetry and their future lives; and although they disagreed on the merits of James Elroy Flecker's *The Golden Journey to Samarkand*, Sassoon particularly enjoyed his junior officer's parody of two lines from this long and popular poem to describe their troops. De Sola Pinto later described Sassoon in his autobiography *The City That Shone*, and his delight in serving with his great poet-hero is very clear. Perceiving that Sassoon was thoroughly bored by the paper-work that reached him every day, de Sola Pinto took on the task of dealing with it for him.

The experience of meeting the German machine-gunners had done nothing to dampen Sassoon's enthusiasm to undertake one more patrol. The Battalion was due to be relieved the next day, 13 July, and as if to ward off evil spirits Sassoon touched the fire-opal that he regarded as 'lucky'. Taking a young corporal (Davies) with him, he set out into No Man's Land. His purpose was to locate a German machine-gun and as they crawled forward, getting within 50 yards of the post, the crew fired a short burst. Crawling a few more yards nearer, both men threw all the hand grenades they were carrying and scurried back to a sunken road where they rested. They had been out well over two hours, and dawn was breaking.

Sassoon had foolishly taken off his heavy steel helmet, and as he stood up he received a glancing blow to the right temple from a British rifle bullet - serious enough, but by great good fortune not mortal. Supported by his corporal, Sassoon staggered back to the Battalion's front line to learn that he had been mistaken for a raider, the explosions of the hand grenades suggesting that a German trench raid was on its way. Although Sassoon's opal had not prevented a near-deadly wound, it brought him the good fortune of a return to England - an outcome which meant that his war was over. From a series of Casualty Clearing Stations and hospitals in France, Sassoon was back in London within

The Royal Welch Fusiliers' sector at Saint Floris, 1918 taken from the approximate location of the German front line in July 1918, looking across No Man's Land towards the British lines. The very effective barrier of the canalised River Lys on the right marked the extreme left of the British front line. Sassoon received his head wound while patrolling in the area to the left of the picture.

a week, in a large hospital ward overlooking Hyde Park. Meanwhile, Lieutenant Jowett and his raiding party of ten men had taken the machine-gun and five German prisoners, the first captured by the 74th Division in France.

VISIT NO. 5 – SAINT VENANT and SAINT FLORIS

This is where Sassoon was in action and shot accidentally by one of his own men. Whilst there are now no traces of the 1918 fighting, a visit to the region will give some idea of the type of terrain which made ordinary trench digging impossible, so that the British had to rely on the less than satisfactory 'grouse butts' for defence.

Leaving the A 26 motorway at Junction no. 5, go round Lillers following signs for Hazebrouck. A left turn, signed Hazebrouck, takes you on to the D 916 road via Busnes (5 km). Continue along this road and about 500 yards beyond a small roundabout take the D 186 road to Saint Floris. The fairly sharp bend in the centre of the village was known to the Royal Welch Fusiliers as 'Hell Fire Corner'. Note the memorials on the church wall beside the war memorial and also the CWGC headstones relating to the Royal Welch casualties from May 1940; one of these was the son of Lieutenant-Colonel Garnett, the Commanding Officer of Sassoon's battalion in the Great War. The general area of the British front line in July 1918 lies to the east; to reach the approximate site, continue along the D 186 for about 1 mile until a small road at the end of the village leads to the canal on the left. (It is possible to drive down here and along to the right, beside the canal.)

Sassoon was wounded in this sector on 13 July 1918.

Chapter Nine

ARMISTICE AND AFTERMATH

Sassoon's wound at St. Floris effectively took him out of the war, just as Graves had been forced out of front-line service by the condition of his lungs after being wounded at Bazentin in July 1916.

One happier occasion in Graves's life had been his marriage in January 1918, although the service itself was not without its dramas.

According to Graves's account in *Goodbye to All That*, it was only on the day of the wedding that Nancy Nicholson realised what she would be expected to commit herself to; after a good deal of protest she went through with the service in conventional manner, but insisted on returning to her land girl's uniform immediately afterwards. Bride and groom were both young (Nancy 18, Robert 22), creative, opinionated and ill-suited to married life on a very small income.

They had known each other for two years, as neighbouring families in the holiday world of North Wales. Nancy's father, William Nicholson, and her older brother Ben were both artists, and Nancy herself had first impressed Graves as more than Ben's younger sister when he saw her in August 1917, during a period of leave and not long after he had seen Sassoon in Craiglockhart. A further meeting in London, in October, confirmed his impression that Nancy shared his attitudes to the war, feminism and to ideas of myth and legend which were to become central to Graves's life. Overall he felt that she represented a happier and more reasonable approach to life than that of his own family. She worked as a land-girl on a farm in Cornwall, and when Robert visited her there in November the love-affair developed. By Christmas they were engaged and decided on an early marriage. Nancy was entirely unconcerned about the need for a wedding ceremony, but recognised that her father would be much upset if she shared her life without marriage; and Robert was anxious for the approval of his own family and friends.

His writing life was also making progress, for the collection of poems *Fairies and Fusiliers*, on which he had been working while at Osborne, was published in the autumn to general acclaim. He had shared with Sassoon in encouraging the new unknown poet Wilfred Owen, who was delighted to be invited to the Graves-Nicholson wedding and to meet more of literary London.

The wedding was followed by a brief week's honeymoon in North

Wales; then Nancy returned to her land-girl life and Robert, though not in particularly robust health, returned to Rhyl and Kinmel Camp, on 1 February 1918. He was now assured of a home posting for the rest of the war, so Nancy was able to join him; and in their happy devotion he was able to write freely, with his imagination moving away from the war and into songs and ballads, more fanciful and free-ranging inventions.

He was not well, however, and in May 1918 (on a visit to London when Ivor Novello considered setting some of the songs to music) his portrait, drawn by the artist Eric Kennington, shows him looking uneasy and unwell. The war experiences haunted him and he sought distraction in impractical plans for a rural idyll in farming.

Grevillers British Cemetery, near Bapaume. The grave of Lieutenant J.A. Nicholson, Nancy Nicholson's brother. In the summer of 1918 their mother contracted Spanish 'flu during her son's leave from France, but neglected the illness to spend more time with him. She died a few days later.

Fate dealt otherwise with them, however. Nancy's beloved mother died of pneumonia - neglected, to avoid spoiling her son Tony's leave. They heard of Sassoon's narrow escape from death, then that her brother Tony had died of wounds, on 5 October. Robert was distressed at the death of Robbie Ross - a staunch literary supporter and guide who had befriended Sassoon, Graves, Wilfred Owen and many others in their social life and literary ambitions. (A quiet, generous and discreet man, he had suffered unwelcome and distressing publicity over a scandalous libel trial. It involved a famous actress and a highly eccentric Member of Parliament, Pemberton Billing, who was convinced that large numbers of the London intelligentsia were (a) homosexual and (b) helping the German war effort.) Then in the early autumn of 1918 Robert's brother Charles almost died of the prevalent Spanish 'flu.

It was not long after Charles's recovery that the Armistice was announced. Thinking back over the horrors of the past four and a half years, Graves reacted with heartfelt bitterness. With the memories of so many dead friends and comrades-in-arms in his mind, he left Kinmel Camp and went out 'walking alone along the dyke above the marshes of Rhuddlan ... cursing and sobbing and thinking of the dead'.

'Somewhere in Kinmel Park'- a war-time photograph showing the camp entrance on the Abergele road.

Kinmel Park Camp, Bodelwyddan, North Wales. A modern military camp exists on the site familiar to Robert Graves. His Officer Cadet battalion occupied barracks some 250 yards to the left of this photograph. The seaside town of Rhyl and the main Crewe-Holyhead railway line, with which the camp railway connected, lie on the skyline.

Meanwhile, Sassoon had spent the final summer of the war, since his lucky escape from death, in London. He recovered slowly from the wound in his head, his recovery perhaps delayed by the swarms of visitors who arrived to see him from his first day in the hospital; not only his mother, but many of his friends in London society or literary life. He was not strong enough to appreciate them, and suffered from fever, sleeplessness, deep feelings of guilt: all visitors were banned for a while. Correspondence with Graves soothed his nervous state, and he sent a verse letter about his wounding. It is an uncharacteristic piece, with his customary irony turned against himself (self-mockery was more usually confined to his diary entries), a confused blend of his current bedridden circumstances and excess of well-wishers, his lucky escape in France and his uncertain state of mind. Written perhaps partly as an explanation to an old friend and partly as a distraction, the piece subsequently led to much bitterness between the two.

169

A visit from Rivers brought him peace of mind, like a father soothing an agitated child. He recovered both physically and emotionally, and returned to poetry to work out his guilt at leaving his men in danger while he was able to escape to England. By mid-August he was able to help Graves with his poetry, suggesting revisions for his next collection. Sassoon's own collection *Counter-Attack* had been receiving high praise, with the notable exception of hostility from John Middleton Murry in *The Nation,* a journal which had printed a number of his poems and which was generally regarded as sympathetic to the more advanced poets of the period.

In the third week of August Sassoon was feeling stronger, and spent a long afternoon with Osbert Sitwell in Chelsea, together with Wilfred Owen, enjoying a dazzling virtuoso music recital, then an indulgent tea and a gentle walk through the delights of the Chelsea Physic Garden. It was a memorable occasion.

The next weeks were spent in London, easing himself back gently into his social and literary world, a Medical Board at Craiglockhart followed by four weeks' leave at Weirleigh, and a visit to Thomas Hardy. Sassoon had admired Hardy for a long time and was delighted with the quietness and restraint that he encountered in the famous poet and novelist. `A great and simple man' was the verdict in Sassoon's diary. Two days later he was in Oxford, and met the poet John Masefield, whom he also liked, and the Poet Laureate, Robert Bridges, who did not impress him. On 11 November he returned to London and,

> *...found masses of people in streets and congested Tubes, all waving flags and making fools of themselves - an outburst of mob patriotism. It was a wretched wet night, and very mild. It is a loathsome ending to the loathsome tragedy of the last four years.*

* * *

Graves and Sassoon both lived long and complex lives after their escape from the First World War, and it is impossible to do more than give the barest outline of some important personalities and events in the ensuing decades. The two men were striking both physically and, in their different ways, intellectually: Graves was tall, rugged, broken-nosed and somewhat flamboyant, with a powerful personal presence, while Sassoon was unusually tall and lean, nervous, self-conscious and self-contained - but both were dedicated to the inner life, always conscious of the importance of literary and spiritual effort and communication. Both men have attracted biographers, literary critics and social historians, their work has become an essential element in studying the First World War and there is a rich supply of sources to be consulted in addition to their own published work (see *Bibliography*, page 187).

Robert Graves's account of his demobilisation in *Goodbye to All That* fits in well with the dark humour that runs through the rest of the book, and seems to be accurate. Having overstayed a leave period in order to be with Nancy when she gave birth to their first child (Jenny, born on 6 January 1919), he travelled to Ireland to rejoin the Third Battalion (the cadet-battalions were now wound up and he was no longer needed at Kinmel Camp) and set about resigning his commission. It seemed advisable to become a student, for he could get a government grant for a two-year course at Oxford, but there were regimental administrative matters to sort out in Limerick first. With determined persuasion, and knowing that he was sickening for a bout of influenza which would be dangerous for his weakened lungs (and which would probably not receive adequate treatment in the local military hospital), he managed to get away on the last available train, for demobilization in Ireland was disallowed because of local troubles. With his papers not quite in order, he decided to take his chance - and by extraordinary coincidence, shared a taxi in London with the only man in the whole British Army who was in a position to provide genuine authorization. He was finally released from the army on 14 February 1919.

Graves reached home, and collapsed with 'flu; the war damage and later illness had damaged his lungs seriously, and he was acutely ill - but recovered, and he and Nancy and their daughter departed to Harlech for several months. This provided a necessary respite and period of recovery, for he was in poor general health, both physically and psychologically and knew that he would not be fit for a normal working life for a long time. He and Nancy were not good at managing their finances, and with royalties coming in from Graves's poetry sales as well as his war bonus and disability pension, together with the prospect of his educational grant to come, they persuaded themselves that they could afford to live without any further income.

University life at Oxford followed, in October 1919, with the young Graves/Nicholson household living at Boar's Hill, outside the city, for the sake of Robert's lungs. He managed to switch from the proposed Classics to English Literature, and became a student at St John's, the college which had accepted him with an Exhibition in 1914.

Sassoon's experience of 1919 also included departure from the British Army - he was demobilized on 11 March - but in other respects it was very different from Graves's life that year. In August 1918 he had spent a restorative period in a large country house in the Scottish borders, where a well-stocked library and peaceful rural surroundings helped him back to physical health and mental stability. His recovery seems to have been helped by the companionship of a fellow-guest and embryonic poet, the Canadian Frank Prewett - known as 'Toronto' from the place of his origins. Sassoon found the younger man attractive, and although it seems unlikely that Prewett returned his affections, the relationship helped Sassoon to accept his homosexual leanings - the cause of much guilt and anguish over the years. His poems from this period contrast strongly with the war poems, for they are more reflective and show his wider personal musings.

Back in London, Sassoon plunged into his busy social life which on this occasion included a first meeting with Winston Churchill, an enjoyable encounter for both men. A further period of rest, this time at home at Weirleigh, followed, with little poetry; he found his mother's somewhat aggressive civilian views on the war difficult to deal with.

It was also at this time that Sassoon met T. E. Lawrence, with whom he could discuss the Middle East and various writers. Lawrence's future fame, and the depths of his character, were not guessed at, but their friendship developed and Sassoon came to a deep admiration of Lawrence's writing. This life of convalescence, musing, literary encounters and occasional poetry went on for several months as he continued on indefinite sick-leave until his demobilization.

Sassoon continued to express his feelings about the war. His poem 'Aftermath' (March 1919) evokes the mental clash between the present-day life of peace and the overpowering memories of war - the conditions of life in the trenches, the rats, the rain and the smell, the anger and the memories that haunted him. The first stanza ends: 'Look down, and swear by the slain of the War that you'll never forget' and the final line provides the echo: 'Look up, and swear by the green of the spring that you'll never forget'.

It was perhaps in this mood that in 1920-21 he collaborated with Edith Sitwell in preparing the publication of a small volume of poems by Wilfred Owen, who in the final months of the war had been gathering work together for a publisher. (More than a decade later Sassoon was to be delighted when his staunch and deeply-admired friend Edmund Blunden undertook a lengthy memoir and fuller edition of Owen's work.)

Among the many differences between Sassoon and Graves, possibly the main divergence was in the different place of creative writing in their lives. Both Sassoon and Graves were deeply interested in the expression of profound human instincts for religious or mystic belief, but over the long post-war decades it became clear that Graves was a prolific, original and professional writer - however wayward his ideas and personality may have appeared at times - while Sassoon found his writing essential to his peace of mind but resisted modernism in literature, a writer by instinct concerned to explore and express his own feelings rather than abstract ideas. Nor did Sassoon generally concern himself with matters outside his direct experience, the place of poetry in 'English Literature' or the importance of literature in the intellectual life.

Human spirituality can take many forms, and for both men their own beliefs were necessary to their thinking and their emotional stability. Graves's application to thought, theory and the techniques of writing poetry helped him to move on and create his own allusive and delicate style, drawing his readers into his internal world. After their war experiences, both men were deeply sympathetic to socialism, a feeling that was widely shared across many levels of society although it also, inevitably, aroused great alarm across the same broad range. Other sympathisers included the Sitwell family, and Virginia and Leonard Woolf. In the early 1920s Sassoon found himself defending striking miners to fellow-members of his London club, while Graves found his egalitarian instincts coinciding with those of his wife Nancy. Sassoon was briefly employed as a journalist with the Daily Herald, although in his case the socialism 'owed nothing to intellectual analysis and everything to his innate sense of justice';[8] he supported the miners in their grievances over pay and conditions and was enraged by the measures to break the General Strike of 1926, but the enthusiasm for greater equality in society waned as he grew older.

The 1920s were marked by the restlessness which afflicted very many of the survivors of the war. Sassoon continued to seem much younger than his real age and, although he spent much of his time alone at his writing desk, in many cases his circle of friends represented the post-war generation. The exceptions were various literary mentors, and the leading writer whose good opinion he most appreciated was Thomas Hardy.

Relationships with war-time friends waxed and waned, depending on mood and chance. Passionate affections and jealousies shaped the moods and complicated his life, for Sassoon was a complex mixture of

[8] *Siegfried Sassoon*, John Stuart Roberts, p.155.

reckless warmth and somewhat prickly self-centredness which must have made him an awkward member of any social circle. His affections tended towards younger men to whom he could be protective; among the more striking and long-lasting of these relationships were the actor Glen Byam Shaw, the artist and socialite Gabriel Atkins and - the most difficult and flamboyant of all - Stephen Tennant. Although he survived to live to a great age, Stephen Tennant suffered from fragile health and was forced to undertake lengthy cures for a tubercular condition.

Sassoon accompanied his young friend on lengthy trips abroad for his health and also did his best to protect him from importunate visitors - none the less, he was a regular visitor to several households where

Sir Edward Grey Foreign Secretary in Asquith's Government later Viscount Grey of Falloden.

the wealthy upper classes indulged in a steady round of travel, weekend house parties and lively social life. The strenuous leisured life of the Edwardians lingered on in this circle and Sassoon was torn between open enjoyment and amusement, a sense of being too old - and somewhat separated from his companions by his war experience - and his personal need for solitude and seclusion in order to write.

If it could be said that Graves's life and work were inseparable, Sassoon struggled to maintain his work and his social life in isolation from each other; it would have been impossible to meet and talk with Graves without recognising him as a writer and thinker, but it must have been entirely possible to engage with Sassoon as a country-dweller, a cricketer and a veteran of the Great War without reference to his poetry.

For several years he lodged in the house of friends in London, and developed a distinctive pattern that suited his social life and his literary inclinations: after sleeping until late in the day he would go out to dine at his club or a restaurant and join his friends, before returning and settling down in quiet solitude to write between midnight and dawn. His poetry showed increasing social comment - the instincts that later turned into his religious thinking and spiritual self-expression - but his writing lacked the energy and drive that had created his war poetry. The poems from this period were 'careful, neat and dead'.[9]

[9] *Ibid*, p.182

TENNANTS AND OTHERS

Stephen Tennant was the son of Lord Glenconner (Eddie Tennant) and his wife Pamela Wyndham. Glenconner's sister Margot was the second wife of Herbert Asquith, the former Prime Minister (his first wife, Helen Kelsall Melland having died of typhoid in 1891). After Eddie's death Pamela married Sir Edward Grey (Viscount Grey of Falloden) who had been Asquith's Foreign Secretary. Asquith's eldest son Raymond, by his first wife, was married to Katharine Horner, and his daughter Violet, also from the first marriage, was married to Maurice Bonham Carter, part of another large political and land-owning family living in the same London and west-country territory. Raymond Asquith and Stephen Tennant's brother Edward Wyndham Tennant (known as Bim) were both killed within a week of each other on the Somme in September 1916, while serving with the Grenadier Guards; they are buried close to each other at Guillemont Road Cemetery. Edward Horner, Katharine's brother, died in November 1917 from wounds received during the Battle of Cambrai, in action with the 18th Hussars.

The extended network of friendships that circled round these interlocking families included Lady Diana Manners, later Lady Diana Cooper, who was a regular correspondent of Raymond Asquith while he was at the front, the artist Rex Whistler (killed in action in July 1944) and, particularly significant for Sassoon, Edith Olivier.

This prosperous set of people was part of Sassoon's social network during the 1920s and 1930s, and their rural settings became his too: the Bonham Carters lived at Stockton in south-west Wiltshire, and Katharine Asquith at Mells, in Somerset. Both places were within easy reach of Sassoon's home - Heytesbury House, in the Wylye Valley; memories of his happy childhood in rural Kent no doubt found echoes in this post-war world.

When the Sassoon marriage ran into serious problems in the 1940s, Hester's mother Katharine Gatty tried to soothe matters. It was through Katharine Asquith, who had become a Roman Catholic in 1924, that Sassoon met Monsignor Ronald Knox, a significant figure in the poet's search for spiritual enlightenment.

Herbert Asquith Prime Minister 1908-16 later Earl of Oxford and Asquith.

Heytesbury House, near Warminster. A modern view of Sassoon's former house.

The constant variety of his social life brought him into a circle of leisured and cultured people who could afford to be self-indulgent. He seems to have found their charmed but restlessly energetic lives both exasperating and irresistible - yet it was within this circle that he found his male emotional relationships, acceptable among his own world but not outside it - and illegal if expressed. The fear of public immorality was overwhelming.

Amidst his turbulent friendships and personal relationships, 1933 was a bad year for Sassoon in which his steady friend Edith Olivier turned his attention to fresh acquaintances. It was through her that he met Hester Gatty, daughter of a successful barrister and, although she was twenty years his junior, he was drawn towards marriage for the first time (apart from the abortive 'understanding' with Bobbie Hanmer's sister many years earlier). They were married at the end of 1933 and moved into Heytesbury House, in Wiltshire, in the spring of 1934

Sassoon's appointment as Literary Editor of *The Herald* in 1919 ultimately required too much of his time but although he eventually gave up the post it brought him at least one good friend. The young war-veteran Edmund Blunden sent him some of his poems, diffidently enquiring whether the Literary Editor would consider them; Sassoon was delighted with the work and, for the rest of his life, found Blunden one of his most enduring friends and rewarding fellow-writers.

After early contentment, the Sassoon marriage was uneasy and grew steadily less satisfactory. The birth of their son George in 1935 brought him tremendous delight, but the personal relationship between Siegfried and Hester deteriorated until the marriage finally broke down irretrievably in the aftermath of the Second World War.

Throughout the 1920s and 1930s Sassoon continued to write poetry, always seeking to express his thoughts and ideas, and his observations on his own life; but he had lost the fire of inspiration that the experience of war had provided and he instinctively resisted modern ideas in poetry, as typified for him by the work of T.S. Eliot. (It is perhaps significant that his journalistic articles in The Herald and The Nation about the clash of ideologies behind the miners' strike in 1920 stirred in him some of the irony and sharpness that had distinguished his war poetry.) The death in June 1922 of his revered father-confessor figure and doctor, William Rivers, deprived him of mature wisdom and guidance and it was not until he found himself able to use his own diaries creatively that he discovered a truly satisfactory and widely-accepted style of expression.

It is one of the interests of Sassoon as a subject for study that he interpreted his life in so many ways - the diaries, the poetry, the fictionalised *Memoirs* and the true autobiography. In 1926 he began to draw on the diary that he had kept for twenty years - half his life-time - and had no difficulty in setting up the framework within which he would present his own experience: nothing of the social and political upheavals of the Edwardian years, nothing about family relationships, his mother shown as 'Aunt Evelyn' with no existence of her own, but plenty about his passions of cricket and hunting and life in the idealised rural world before the Great War. He found it an immensely satisfying book to write and, apart from a period of writer's block caused by a period of disturbance in his emotional life, completed it for publication in 1928. His mother's unstinting approval gave him particular pleasure, and the book was indeed an immediate and considerable success.

He followed it in due course with *Memoirs of an Infantry Officer*, continuing with the same device of using fictional names for real people who are nonetheless fairly easily recognisable; the book covers the momentous events of 1916 and 1917. The third volume (a projected fourth was never written) was *Sherston's Progress* which dealt with the period of his famous 'Statement', the time at Craiglockhart and his movements in the final year of the war. It was published in 1936, and was followed by the volumes of unmediated autobiography.

Sassoon's friendship with Blunden, which began after the war but which was intensified by experiences that both recalled with horror, endured with very few periods of coolness; but the initially very close and supportive friendship with Graves died away after the publication of *Goodbye to All That*. It revived from time to time, generally when Graves, the more outward looking of the two, made contact, but lapsed again. Money was a bone of contention - loans requested by Graves and sometimes sent, awkwardness in Graves's expression of gratitude or resentment on Sassoon's part - but he was delighted when the news of Sassoon's religious conversion brought a letter from Graves, after a long period of estrangement .

THE IMPORTANCE OF GOOD TIMING ...

The authors of the three greatest literary memoirs of the First World War - Sassoon with his *Memoirs*, Graves with *Goodbye to All That*, Blunden with *Undertones of War* - make an interesting trio to compare. All three were committed to writing poetry before the war began, although Graves and Blunden went straight from school to the trenches, but it took all of them around a decade to produce their enduring prose record of life at war. All three were marked for life by their war-time life and were aware that those years had affected them profoundly. They knew each other well, although their sympathies wavered from time to time - both Sassoon and, particularly, Graves were difficult people to get on with; Blunden was steadier in temperament and in his support for Sassoon but even he found Graves an impossible friend at times.

Whereas Blunden and Sassoon used their own diaries to create as accurate a record as possible, Graves was not averse to giving offence with *Goodbye to All That*. It was intended as an autobiography - although he was only 34 - and was written at a time when he urgently needed to make money, and had a sick wife, four young children and no reliable income. The opening paragraph gives the objects of the book as 'an opportunity for a formal goodbye to ... all that', for he was about to leave England to teach abroad. He wrote later that he had taken care to put in plenty of popular ingredients, including murders, ghosts, school life, love affairs, wounds, weddings, religious doubts and, 'the best bet of all', battles.

War poetry had been immensely popular during the war and for a short time after it, before fading in public demand (as Graves predicted); and several years were needed before the experience of the war was sufficiently digested to be recreated on paper rather than in nightmares and nervous disturbance. The nightmares proved to be a life-time's legacy, but in due course they could be interpreted for others to read about. The late 1920s saw a surge in interpretations of the war that included R.C.Sherriff's play *Journey's End* as well as the three classic personal memoirs.

Part of the success of Sassoon's three volumes of memoirs probably lies in the skilful presentation by an apparently very straightforward narrator. To this can be added his evocation of childhood and the vivid descriptions of scenes and incidents, both before the war and during it; relationships are equally straightforward, personalities richly described with humour and dark irony. A steady thread of self-deprecation makes the narrator an attractive character. It is only on fuller consideration that Sassoon's own self-centredness can be discerned, his resistance to independent maturity and his lack of insight into other people's feelings or attitudes, characteristics that became stronger as he aged.

Although his war poetry had been widely acclaimed (*The Old Huntsman in 1917* and *Counter-Attack* in 1918), his later poems did not find such favour. Echoes of the war emerged in some later poetry; 'On Passing the New Menin Gate' for example (begun in July 1927, finished six months later) expresses his rage and horror at the endless 'intolerably nameless names' on the great new monument to the missing of the battles of Ypres. Death, he felt, was properly registered individually, as he had felt hit by the death of David Thomas and other specific friends, rather than in a mass of names so numerous that they lost all human singularity. His much-loved expression of a lifting of spirits after the Armistice came in 'Everyone Sang', written in April 1919 - a poem which apparently came to him unexpectedly and virtually ready-made.

After the enormous and sustained success of the 'Sherston' volumes, he drew again on his own life in the autobiographical *The Old Century, The Weald of Youth,* and *Siegfried's Journey*, published between 1938 and 1945. These gave far more of his London social and intellectual life, filling in the omissions of the earlier fictionalised memoirs.

In the descent towards war in the late 1930s Sassoon, like so many other veterans of 1914-18, felt almost paralysed by despair. The war itself was painful, his marriage deteriorated and his handsome house became shabby and uncomfortable. The post-war years were also unsatisfactory for Sassoon, both personally and in his literary life; the greyness and discomforts of the late 1940s and the 1950s found him alone in Heytesbury, sparsely furnished since his wife's departure with her own possessions. Later she went to live in the Isle of Mull, where their son George generally joined her in his holidays from boarding school - and so Sassoon saw less of his son than he would have wished. His health became less robust.

There were friends for whom he was constant and who brought him delight, particularly in cricket and in recalling the 1914-1918 war, but his complex and rigidly self-focussed life made him a difficult man to engage with or help in sustaining his household. Intensely private and insisting on maintaining his ways - to the extent of excluding many who wished him well - but lonely and unable to share in the modern world, he finally found the answer to his quest for fulfilment in the Catholic church. In 1957 his long friendship with Edmund Blunden was revived after a period of coolness, coinciding with recognition of his ultimate spiritual quest. This found expression through some remarkable women - Mother Margaret Mary in London and, later, Dame Felicitas Corrigan, Mother Superior of Stanbrook Abbey, an enclosed convent in Worcestershire. Friendship with Monsignor Ronald Knox and with Downside Abbey led him to conversion and his reception into the Catholic faith.

The Church brought him great joy and peace; his poetry and thinking now turned to exploring and expressing his faith and he longed to share his experience with others. He died in September 1957, and was buried in the parish church at Mells, close to the grave of Ronald Knox.

In the difficult post-war years, both men were similar to many thousands of war veterans, unable to find their way in life, unhappy and frequently angry. While Sassoon sought restlessly for friendship, circling endlessly round his own feelings and returning to his own past, Graves plunged into literary life, moved away from his early life and the war and advanced on life across a broad creative front; first, however, he had to establish himself as a civilian adult.

The Manor House at Mells, home of the Earl of Oxford and Asquith. Towards the end of his life Sassoon would visit Katharine Horner, who lived here until her death in 1976 at the age of 90. She was the widow of Raymond Asquith, who was killed on the Somme in September 1916 and is commemorated in Mells church (seen here). Sassoon is buried in the churchyard.

His family life was never straightforward. A demanding but attractive character, convoluted and extreme, he had a talent for upsetting everyone around him. Existence after the war was a sequence of financial and personal upsets; a small shop that he and Nancy ran at Boar's Hill outside Oxford, when his undergraduate days were over, failed for lack of capital and good management, and life became a permanent struggle against poverty, Nancy's poor health and Robert's determination to live off his writing as well as coping with most of the household management. Out of loyalty and friendship Sassoon lent them money from time to time, but the friendship was more difficult now and Sassoon and Nancy never managed to get on comfortable terms with each other. Although he occasionally contributed to the young couple's finances, they frequently had to seek financial support from their parents.

The grave of Siegfried Sassoon at Mells.

Life in the 1920s was shaped by several sets of challenging circumstances. Intellectually, Robert could only see himself engaged in a professional career as a poet and writer; but he was committed to his wife and their young family emotionally and practically - desperately needed by them and equally dependent on their need for him and his part in their welfare - while mentally he was nervous and easily over-wrought. Nancy had borne four children in less than five years and was not skilled at household management. After the disastrous shop-keeing venture they moved to Islip, an isolated village where Robert's mother Amy bought them the cottage of their dreams; but their income was so small and unreliable that they were often hungry and could never be sure of paying their rent or other day-to-day needs.

Nancy Nicholson, Robert's wife, in the mid-1920s.

Robert was often in sole charge of running the household, and found great happiness in caring for the children - but was unable to give more than snatched and unpredictable bursts of attention to his writing. As in his school and army days, he quarrelled easily with family and friends and supported his wife against the world

in her stalwart independence of mind and her social lack of ease.

Two unexpected deaths in quick succession in 1922 - Dr Rivers (Sassoon's doctor at Craiglockhart, with whom Graves had had long and fruitful conversations to exorcise the after-effects of the war) and Sir Walter Raleigh, Graves's mentor at Oxford University - were a severe shock and deprived him of much-needed and valued support. He did however achieve some literary publications: *Oxford Poetry 1921*, which he edited, and *On English Poetry* in the same year. His own poetry had moved away from direct reference to the war, although some of the poems in *Whipperginny* (1923) and *Mockbeggar Hall* (1926) were haunted by sinister past experience.

After delays (and much anxiety and nervous agitation) Graves successfully gained his B.Litt. degree in 1925. Despite urgings and practical guidance from his father, he was reluctant to seek regular employment in the literary world, and indeed his health concerns and the domestic demands of his family made him an unlikely prospect. Nancy's health and emotional stability were also very precarious and eventually both were warned that she needed to be in a warm climate. Of two job offers that reached him, the Professorship of English at Cairo University was particularly attractive, although during the long wait for confirmation of the post he was forced to seek financial help yet again from his parents and from Sassoon.

Despite all the domestic difficulties Robert had by now written a significant amount of his finest poetry and was ready for a wider world: the young family sailed for Cairo at the end of 1925. They travelled in the company of a new acquaintance, the controversial young American poet Laura Riding. Graves had a high opinion of her work and they had already corresponded for some time while she, recently divorced, was anxious to collaborate with him on a book on modern poetry.

Apart from the immediate relief of financial pressures and the longer improvement in Nancy's health, however, the Cairo position was not a success. Graves and the University did not suit each other, the extended household returned to England before the end of the year - and by now Robert was in love with Laura.

Their lives were sustained by the successful publication in 1927 of Graves's biography of his friend T. E. Lawrence (*Lawrence and the Arabs*) but the situation evolved until in 1928 Graves and Riding were living together while Nancy and the children lived in a barge on the Thames. This was extended a year later with the addition of Geoffrey Phibbs, an Irish writer who also fell under the spell of Laura's

dominating and manipulative personality

The uncomfortable quartet collapsed at Easter 1929 when Laura Riding made a dramatic suicide bid and was severely injured, closely followed by Graves who suffered lesser injuries. Phibbs and Nancy decided to live together, leaving Laura with Robert as her devoted and unquestioning lover and companion. Early that summer, he began on his, *Goodbye to All That*.

To some extent it could be said that his brilliantly effective style - straightforward, brisk, vivid, unpretentious - added to the difficulties that he created for himself in his presentation of historical detail. Writing under Laura Riding's influence (which profoundly coloured his attitude to his family and his own past), he was deeply conscious of the divided loyalties in his domestic life and by the clash of beliefs within his wider family. The result was a cynicism and reconstruction of the past which extended to factually verifiable facts, belying the genuinely high-minded morality of his original approach to the war. The untreated shell-shock which affected him throughout the 1920s also affected his memory and interpretation of factual events - intensified by his declaration, dating from earlier in the decade, that 'literal truth is relatively unimportant, as an artist can tell the truth by a condensation and dramatisation of the facts'.[10]

Graves was apparently not worried at causing offence with *Goodbye to All That*. The University and Public Schools battalions, Scots and Scottish regiments and the Cheshire Regiment all had reason to complain. Some did so, and he met their criticisms in his book *But It Still Goes on*, and in the press. Along the way he misrepresented his parents - and thereby added to their sense of weary despair over him; but he had at last discovered how to get away from all the elements in his life which, he felt, had complicated his restoration to mental and human balance since the war; and even, perhaps his childhood and schooldays.

Robert Graves' frontispiece of *Goodbye To All That*.

The book was also written at great speed, with much of it completed within three months, giving little time to check facts. Despite its many factual inaccuracies, and the great offence that he caused to friends and other war veterans, the book has survived as a strikingly honest description of what it felt like to take part in the First World War and how the author

[10] Biographies of Graves give considerable space to the circumstances surrounding the publication of *Goodbye To All That* (see bibliography).

looked back at it, a decade later.

Among those who were upset were Edmund Blunden (who felt that he misrepresented atmosphere and detail) and most of his Royal Welch Fusilier comrades - in particular, Siegfried Sassoon. The inclusion of Sassoon's personal letter-poem, written in some distress in 1918 and beginning: 'I'd timed my death in action to the minute', and the passage on spiritualism in the Sassoon household, caused particular offence and when Sassoon saw a review copy he insisted on alterations. The first edition therefore appeared with blank spaces replacing the poem and the passage on the spiritualist séance.

Sassoon and Blunden went through the book, comparing notes and noting the inaccuracies or discrepancies - although, later, Blunden at least felt somewhat apologetic at their somewhat childish picking over of the details. Finally, in their exchange of letters in 1957 (just after a revised reissue of Graves's book), Sassoon admitted that he had been in a 'great state of mental fatigue and worry' when *Goodbye* first appeared. He also acknowledged the generosity of Graves's descriptions of himself.

The book, published in November 1929, was a tremendous and immediate success - indeed, the controversy that it aroused, and the consequent flood of letters and articles in newspapers of all levels, added greatly to the author's fame, or notoriety. Coinciding with the offence caused in many directions by the irregularity of his domestic life - the complicated imbroglio with Laura, Nancy and Geoffrey Phibbs - Robert's overwhelming devotion to Laura Riding led to a situation of estrangement from his entire family. An apology of a sort for the inaccuracies in *Goodbye*, published in the Times Literary Supplement, cited the conditions that he suffered in the war as the main cause.

By then, however, the uncompromising and unconventional pair of poets had reached Mallorca and the village of Deyá. Apart from the decade that covered the Spanish Civil War and the Second World War, when he returned to England (Laura having by now departed back to the United States), the household that they created here was to be Graves's home for the rest of his life.

The Seizin Press, a publishing venture founded by Graves and Riding in 1928 and developed in Deyá, was a long-term venture into hand printing and publishing which released the pair from the need to negotiate with hostile or reluctant publishers. It became a significant element in his life, a reliable source for many readers of Graves's thinking and poetry, and part of his legacy to his family.

It continued to be a varied and productive life, both domestically and in literary terms: after Laura Riding's final repudiation of Graves in 1940 and her return to the United States, Graves married Beryl Hodge, with whom he had a further four children. Graves's charismatic character and the house in Deyá became a focus for students and aspiring poets, and for the 'muses' – a sequence of young women who for Graves represented the female principle that underlay his theories of human instinctive knowledge and belief, and inspired his poetry. Influenced perhaps by his devotion to his mother and part of his unswerving subservience to Laura, he was convinced that human society was based on an originally matriarchal foundation. This approach to poetry and human relationships led to the publication in 1948 of *The White Goddess*, his synthesis of the 'historical grammar of poetic myth' and the core of human belief systems.

He was a prolific writer over the years, and his output of poetry, short stories, historical novels (based on various periods of history, including the Roman Empire account *I Claudius* which was televised with great success in the 1970s) and *Goodbye to All That* sold well. Although his theories of female mysticism and myth were questioned – particularly when he was seen to add his endorsement to ideas of youthful rebellion in the 1960s – he added to his income with annual lecture tours in the U.S.A. The myths of ancient Greece and Rome further fuelled his writing and lecturing; later literary critics recognise his influence on many poets and their work. In 1961-65 he was Visiting Professor of Poetry at Oxford University, attracting vast audiences for his lectures, but by the early 1970s he was retreating into a state of

Robert Graves in 1940.

mental confusion. Physically he remained strong for rather longer, but in his mind he was often back in the First World War. Guilt at the deaths for which he had been responsible overcame him: in 1979 he stated to a visitor that 'I am in Hell' and for the final five years of his life all mental understanding was gone. Robert Graves died in December 1985 and is buried in Deyá.

* * *

The long lives of Robert Graves and Siegfried Sassoon, these two challenging and gifted characters, were shaped by what they saw, did and understood in the First World War. In a short guide it is impossible to do full justice to their work and their contribution to our understanding of what they lived through but, more than a century since their birth, they undoubtedly still have fresh insights to offer. The richness and complexity of their minds, their prose and their poetry take the reader far beyond the basic facts of war.

BIBLIOGRAPHY

Goodbye to All That, Robert Graves, Jonathan Cape, 1929; reissued with alterations, Cassell 1957; Penguin Books 1984

Good-Bye to All That. An Autobiography, edited, with a biographical essay and annotations by Richard Perceval Graves. Berghahn Books, Oxford 1995

But it Still Goes On, Robert Graves Jonathan Cape London 1930

Poems about War, Robert Graves, Cassell, 1988

Robert Graves. The Assault Heroic 1895-1926, Richard Perceval Graves Weidenfeld & Nicolson, 1986

Robert Graves: The Years with Laura 1926-1940, Richard Perceval Graves, Weidenfeld & Nicolson, 1990

Robert Graves: A Life on the Edge, Miranda Seymour, Doubleday, 1995

In Broken Images. Selected Letters of Robert Graves, 1914-1946, ed. Paul O'Prey, Hutchinson, 1982

The War Poems of Siegfried Sassoon, Faber & Faber, 1983

Collected Poems, Siegfried Sassoon, Faber & Faber, 1947

The Sherston Memoirs, Siegfried Sassoon, 1936

Memoirs of a Fox-Hunting Man, Siegfried Sassoon, Faber & Faber, 1928

Memoirs of an Infantry Officer, Siegfried Sassoon, Faber & Faber, 1930

Sherston's Progress, Siegfried Sassoon, Faber & Faber, 1936

Diaries, 1915-1918, Siegfried Sassoon, ed. Rupert Hart-Davis, Faber & Faber, 1983

The Old Century and Seven More Years, Siegfried Sassoon, Faber & Faber, 1938

The Weald of Youth, Siegfried Sassoon, Faber & Faber, 1942

Siegfried's Journey, Siegfried Sassoon, Faber & Faber, 1945

Siegfried Sassoon. The Making of a War Poet, A Biography. 1886-1918, Jean Moorcroft Wilson. Duckworth & Co.Ltd., London. 1998.

Siegfried Sassoon 1886-1967 John Stuart Roberts, Richard Cohen Books, London 1999

Siegfried Sassoon: Scorched Glory, a critical study, Paul Moeyes, Macmillan, 1997

The Great War and Modern Memory, Paul Fussell, OUP, 1975

Regimental Records of the Royal Welch Fusiliers (23rd Foot), Vol.III.1914-1918, C.H.Dudley Ward, Forster Groom & Co. Ltd., London. 1928

The Sussex Yeomanry and 16th (Sussex Yeomanry) Battalion Royal Sussex Regiment 1914-1919, H.I. Powell-Edwards, Andrew Melrose Ltd. London. 1921

A History of the British Cavalry 1816-1919. Vol. 8 The Western Front 1915-1918, Epilogue 1919-1939. The Marquess of Anglesey, Leo Cooper, Barnsley. 1997

Cotton Town Comrades, Mitchinson & McInnes. Bayonet Publications 1993

The West Yorkshire Regiment in the War 1914-1918 Vol I Wyrall, John Lane The Bodley Head Ltd. London

The Roll Of Honour and War Record of the Artists' Rifles. Anon. Howlett & Son London. 1922

A Brief Record of The Advance of the Egyptian Expeditionary Force under the Command of General Sir Edmund H.H.Allenby, Government Press, Cairo. 1919

Allenby Brian Gardner. Cassell & Co. Ltd, London. 1965

Owen Roscomyl & The Welsh Horse, Bryn Owen, Palace Books, Caernarfon. 1990

A Companion to The British Army 1660-1983, David Ascoli, Book Club Associates, London. 1984

The War the Infantry Knew 1914-1919, Captain J. C. Dunn, P.S.King Ltd., 1938; reissued, Jane's Publishing Co.Ltd., London. 1987

On the Trail of the Poets of the Great War - Wilfred Owen, Helen McPhail & Philip Guest, Leo Cooper, Barnsley. 1998

On the Trail of the Poets of the Great War - Edmund Blunden, Helen McPhail & Philip Guest, Leo Cooper, Barnsley. 1999

Diana Cooper, Philip Ziegler. Hamish Hamilton, London. 1981

The Letters of T.E.Lawrence, ed. Malcolm Brown, J.M.Dent & Sons Ltd., London. 1988

The Balloonatics, Alan Morris, Jarrolds Ltd. London. 1970.

Unquiet Souls, Angela Lambert, Harper & Row, New York. 1984

Shot At Dawn, Julian Putkowski & Julian Sykes Wharncliffe Publishing Ltd., Barnsley. 1989

The Kinmel Park Camp Riots 1919, Julian Putkowski, Flintshire Historical Society. 1989

Stand To! The Journal of the Western Front Association   No. 32. Summer 1991

Mametz. Lloyd George's "Welsh Army" at the Battle of the Somme, Colin Hughes, Orion Press. 1985

Nothing of Importance, Bernard Adams, Gliddon Books, Norwich. 1979

Up To Mametz, Wyn Griffith. Gliddon Books. Norwich. 1988

Armageddon Road - Billy Congreve, Terry Norman, ed., Wm. Kimber & Co Ltd., London 1983

The Hell They Called High Wood, Terry Norman, ed., Wm. Kimber & Co.Ltd. London. 1984

David Jones - A Fusilier at the Front, Anthony Hyne, Poetry Wales Press Ltd. Bridgend. 1995

Mediterranean Submarines, M.Wilson & P.Kemp, Crecy Publishing Ltd. Wilmslow, Cheshire. 1997

British Regiments 1914-18, E.A.James, Samson Books. London. 1978

Mametz Wood, Michael Renshaw, Pen & Sword, Barnsley. 1999

Fricourt - Mametz, Michael Stedman, Pen & Sword, Barnsley. 1997

INDEX

The names of Robert Graves and Siegfried Sassoon, and references to the 1st and 2nd Royal Welch Fusiliers, appear throughout the text.